Presented To:

_____

Presented By:

_____

Date:

_____

God's Little Devotional Book

Honor Books
Tulsa, Oklahoma

2nd Printing

God's Little Devotional Book
ISBN 1-56292-977-1
Copyright © 1995, 2001 by Honor Books, Inc.
P.O. Box 55388
Tulsa, Oklahoma 74155

Introduction

Everyone can use a little inspiration, a little reminder of what is truly good, moral and just. *God's Little Devotional Book* provides just that!

These devotionals—linked to pithy quotations and also to verses from the Bible—are short and easy-to-read . . . but no less meaningful. You'll find anecdotes, illustrations, and stories that make you laugh, challenge you to think, and in some cases, touch the soft spot of your heart. As one reader has said, "Some of these hit me right between the eyes . . . and others caused tears to come to my eyes." Either way, this book promises you an expanded vision and new insights. And because the devotionals are tied to the external truth of God's Word, they also will help build in you excellence of character and strength of integrity.

God's Little Devotional Book is for readers of all ages, in all circumstances of life, in all professions. These devotionals are ones to which virtually every person can relate, and from which every person can draw encouragement. They'll add meaning to your day with truth, even as they brighten your day with hope! Share them with your children. Share them with a friend. They're guaranteed to offer a road map to succeed in the daily journey of life!

> *A marriage may be made in heaven, but the maintenance must be done on earth*

A woman once went away on a long weekend retreat with a group of women from her church. About halfway through the final Monday-morning session, she suddenly jumped to her feet and left the room. Concerned, a friend followed her to see what had caused her to leave the meeting so abruptly. She found her friend just as she was hanging up a telephone in the lobby.

"Is everything all right?" she asked urgently.

"Oh, yes," the woman responded. "I didn't mean to cause you alarm." A bit sheepishly, she added, "I suddenly remembered that it's Monday morning—trash day."

"Trash day? Your husband is still at home. Surely . . . "

"Yes," the woman interrupted, "but it takes two of us to put out the trash. I can't carry it. And he can't remember it."

Marriages are meant to be complementary—two pulling together as one, not in competition, but in mutual association. Learning how to work together and how to live together is the "maintenance" of love.

Nevertheless let every one of you in particular so love his wife even as himself; and the wife see that she reverence her husband.
EPHESIANS 5:33

President Lincoln had a disarming and engaging ability to laugh at himself, especially his own physical appearance. When Senator Stephen A. Douglas once called him a "two-faced man," Lincoln responded, "I leave it to my audience. If I had another face, do you think I would wear this one?"

Another time he told a group of editors about meeting a woman riding on horseback in the wood. She "looked at me intently, and said, 'I do believe you are the ugliest man I ever saw.' Said I, 'Madam, you are probably right, but I can't help it.' 'No,' she said, 'you can't help it, but you might stay at home.'"

When God measures a man, he puts the tape around the heart instead of the head.

Although his likeness is widely recognized, Lincoln is not known primarily for his appearance, but for his courageous stance for restoration of the Union and the abolition of slavery. He is often held up as an example of remarkable patience, determination, dedication, strong will, compassion, thoughtfulness, and selflessness. These inner qualities are what mark Lincoln as one of America's greatest presidents.

So much is made in our culture today of outward appearance and material possessions. We do well to remember that it is our virtuous inner qualities that create a lasting reputation.

The Lord seeth not as man seeth; for man looketh on the outward appearance, but the Lord looketh on the heart.
1 SAMUEL 16:7

> *The grass may look greener on the other side, but it still has to be mowed.*

A stonecutter once delivered a slab of stone to a merchant. Seeing all his wonderful goods, he said, "I wish I was a merchant and had such things." In the twinkling of an eye, his wish was granted. Then one day he saw a parade pass his store window. He saw a prince pass by in splendor and he said, "I wish I was a prince." And immediately he became a prince . . . until the day the hot sun beat down upon him and he said, "I wish I was the sun, greater than any man." And he became the sun and was happy . . . until a cloud came between him and the earth. He said, "That cloud overshadows me. I wish I was a cloud." Again his wish was granted. He rained down on the earth to his heart's content until he came to a mountain, which wouldn't let him pass. He said, "That mountain is greater than I. I wish I was a mountain." Instantly, he became a mountain and he thought, *Now I am the greatest of all.*

But one day a little man climbed up the mountain and with a hammer and chisel began to tap away at it. The mountain, unable to stop him, said, "That little man is greater than I. I wish I was a man who cut stone." Once again his wish was granted and he became a stonecutter. He lived a long and useful life and everyone marveled at how happy he was.

Be content with such things as ye have . . .
HEBREWS 13:5

An old train on a branch line was puffing and creaking slowly through the countryside when suddenly it lurched to a stop. The only passenger in the three-car train rose quickly to his feet and hurried to find the conductor. "Why have we stopped?" he demanded. "I'm a salesman, and I have an appointment in less than an hour in the next town. Surely this old train can make it through a pasture!"

The conductor smiled, "Nothing to worry about sir. Just a cow on the tracks. Gotta wait her out." The salesman returned to his seat, fuming and fidgeting until the train began to creep forward again after about ten minutes. It chugged along for a mile or two and then ground to a halt once again.

Patience is the ability to keep your motor idling when you feel like stripping your gears.

This time the conductor found the salesman. "Don't worry," he said. "We'll be on our way shortly. It's just a temporary delay." The exasperated salesman asked, "What now? Did we catch up to the cow again?"

What this salesman didn't know was that the schedule for this particular train had been made so as to allow for temporary delays and cows on the track! The salesman made his appointment, but he was worn to a frazzle by his own frustration and concern.

Allow for delays. You'll enjoy life's journey more.

He that is slow to anger is better than the mighty; and he that ruleth his spirit than he that taketh a city.

PROVERBS 16:32

GLDB

> *He who is waiting for something to turn up might start with his own shirt sleeves.*

Many people remember President Theodore Roosevelt as an avid hunter and sportsman. Few, however, know of his efforts for conservation, which is a far greater legacy.

After a hunting trip to the Dakota region in 1887—years before he was president—Roosevelt returned to his East coast home reporting that trees were being cut down carelessly, animals were being slaughtered by "swinish game-butchers," and that the wilderness was in danger. He expressed great shock at how quickly this region that he loved was being stripped of its glory—the big game gone, the ponds drying up, the beavers disappearing, the grasslands becoming desert.

But Roosevelt did more than talk. He founded the Boone and Crockett Club, dedicated to the preservation of wilderness in America. Largely through that club's influence, legislation was passed to care for Yellowstone National Park, to protect sequoia trees in California, to set aside nature reserves for bird and sea life, and to limit the shooting of big game. Laws were also passed to regulate hunting practices.

Hoping for change rarely brings about change. Work, however, generally does!

All hard work brings a profit, but mere talk leads only to poverty.

PROVERBS 14:23 (NIV)

Few sights evoke as much attention, and awe, as that of a large flock of Canadian geese winging their way in their V-formation to the north or south. They speak of the changing of seasons, and also of the value of teamwork.

What many don't know is that when a goose gets sick, or perhaps is wounded by a shot, it never falls from formation by itself. Two other geese also fall out of formation with it and follow the ailing goose down to the ground. One of them is very often the mate of the wounded bird, since geese mate for life and are extremely loyal to their mates. Once on the ground, the healthy birds help protect the goose and care for it as much as possible, even to the point of throwing themselves between the weakened bird and

Remember the banana— when it left the bunch, it got skinned.

possible predators. They stay with the goose until it is either able to fly, or until it is dead. Then, and only then, do they launch out on their own. In most cases, they wait for another group of geese to fly overhead and join them, adding to the safety and flying efficiency of their numbers.

If only we human beings would care for one another this well! Stick with your friends, . . . and more importantly, stick by them.

Not forsaking the assembling of ourselves together, as the manner of some is; but exhorting one another: and so much the more, as ye see the day approaching.
HEBREWS 10:25

> *It is better to be silent and be considered a fool than to speak and remove all doubt.*

William Penn, leader of the early American colonists who eventually named their state of Pennsylvania in his honor, gave these rules regarding conversation:

"Avoid company where it is not profitable or necessary, and in those occasions, speak little, and last.

"Silence is wisdom where speaking is folly, and always safe.

"Some are so foolish as to interrupt and anticipate those who speak instead of hearing and thinking before they answer, which is uncivil, as well as silly.

"If thou thinkest twice before thou speakest once, thou wilt speak twice the better for it.

"Better to say nothing than not to the purpose. And to speak pertinently, consider both what is fit, and when it is fit, to speak.

"In all debates, let truth be thy aim, not victory or an unjust interest; and endeavor to gain, rather than to expose, thy antagonist."

Yea also, when he that is a fool walketh by the way, his wisdom faileth him, and he saith to every one that he is a fool.
ECCLESIASTES 10:3

At one point during his youth, baseball great Jackie Robinson began to run with a neighborhood gang. In later years, he recalled that while he had *wished* for a better life as a boy and teen, he had no understanding that a gang was not the way to achieve it. An older friend finally came to Jackie and made him realize how much he was hurting his hard-working mother, as well as how much he was limiting himself. Robinson said, "He told me that it didn't take guts to follow the crowd, that courage and intelligence lay in being willing to be different."

Many a good man has failed because he had his wishbone where his backbone should have been.

Jackie listened, left the gang, and traded his wishbone for a backbone. He began to work on developing his own physical potential and within a few short years, became a sensational athlete. Starring in football, basketball, baseball and track at UCLA, he was the first person to win athletic awards in all four sports at the university. He went on to play pro football with the Los Angeles Bulldogs before being drafted for World War II duty. After the war, he signed with the Brooklyn Dodgers. Not only did Jackie Robinson become the first black baseball player in the major leagues, but he was voted rookie of the year.

Backbone accomplishes more than wishbone!

Have not I commanded thee? Be strong
and of good courage; be not afraid,
neither be thou dismayed; for the Lord
thy God is with thee withersoever thou goest.
JOSHUA 1:9

> *If at first you don't succeed, try reading the instructions.*

A young ensign had nearly completed his first overseas tour of duty when he was given an opportunity to display his ability at getting the ship under way. With a stream of crisp commands, he had the decks buzzing with men, and soon the ship had left port and was steaming out of the channel.

The ensign's efficiency had been remarkable. In fact, the deck was abuzz with talk that he had set a new record for getting a destroyer under way. The ensign glowed at his accomplishment and was not all that surprised when another seaman approached him with a message from the captain. He was, however, a bit surprised to find that it was a *radio* message, and he was even more surprised when he read, "My personal congratulations upon completing your underway preparation exercise according to the book and with amazing speed. In your haste, however, you have overlooked one of the unwritten rules—make sure the captain is aboard before getting under way."

God's Manual for Life, the Bible, is our "set of instructions" for getting our lives under way. But we must never become so bound to the book that we forget the Author of it and the relationship He desires to have with us on the voyage.

Take fast hold of instruction; let her not go: keep her; for she is thy life.
PROVERBS 4:13

When a person loses his temper, one of the most common expressions used to describe the situation is "fly off the handle." This phrase refers to the head of a hammer coming loose from its handle as the carpenter attempts to use it. Several things happen as a result:

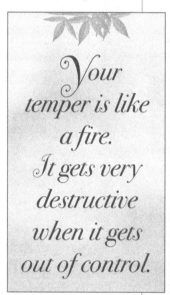

Your temper is like a fire. It gets very destructive when it gets out of control.

- First, the hammer becomes useless—no longer good for work. In like manner, when a person loses his temper, he often loses his effectiveness. Anything he says may not be taken seriously and is likely to be unproductive.

- Second, the hammerhead—twirling out of control—is likely to cause some type of damage to anything in its path. The people who lose their temper cause damage even if they don't realize it—perhaps physically to people or objects in their way, and nearly always emotionally to others who feel they are victims of uncontrolled wrath.

- Third, the repair of both the hammer and the resulting damage takes time. The people who lose their tempers may recover quickly, but the one who is the victim of a hot temper rarely recovers as quickly.

Keep your temper today. Nobody else wants it.

He that hath no rule over his own spirit is like a city that is broken down, and without walls.
PROVERBS 25:28

> *Decisions can take you out of God's will but never out of His reach.*

In her book, *A Closer Walk,* author Catherine Marshall tells about a great personal struggle she experienced after writing a novel titled *Gloria.* Marshall began the novel in 1969 and then abandoned the project two-and-a-half years later. To her, the shelved manuscript was "like a death in the family."

In attempting to reconcile her conflicting thoughts and feelings, Marshall spent time at a retreat house in Florida. While there, she reread a Bible story from Numbers about a time when poisonous snakes filled the Israelite camp. The people recognized the snakes as punishment for their sin, and cried out in repentance. The Lord told Moses to "make a [bronze] snake and put it up on a pole; anyone who is bitten can look at it and live" (Numbers 21:9, NIV).

Marshall realized that just as the Israelites took that which had hurt them, lifted it up to God, and were healed, so we each can take our mistakes and sins, lift them to God in prayer, and trust Him to heal us. She writes, "When any one of us has made a wrong (or even doubtful) turning in our lives through arrogance or lack of trust or impatience or fear—God will show us a way out." Even when we stray, He knows both where we are and how to get us back on His path.

If we are faithless, he will remain faithful, for he cannot disown himself.
2 TIMOTHY 2:13 (NIV)

A scorpion, being a very poor swimmer, once asked a turtle to carry him on his back across the river. "Are you mad?" exclaimed the turtle. "You'll sting me while I'm swimming and I'll drown."

The scorpion laughed as he replied, "My dear turtle, if I were to sting you, you would drown and I would go down with you. Now, what would be the point of that? I won't sting you. It would mean my own death!"

The turtle thought about the logic of his argument for a few moment and then said, "You're right. Hop on!" The scorpion climbed aboard and halfway across the river, he gave the turtle a mighty sting.

As the turtle began to sink to the bottom of the river with the scorpion on its back, it

Your companions are like the buttons on an elevator. They will either take you up or they will take you down.

moaned in dismay, "After your promise, you still stung me! Why did you do that? Now, we're both doomed."

The drowning scorpion sadly replied, "I couldn't help it. It's my nature to sting."

Study the character of a person before you make them a friend. The stage on which their character plays is going to be your life!

He that walketh with wise men shall be wise: but a companion of fools shall be destroyed.
PROVERBS 13:20

GLDB

> *Patience is a quality you admire in the driver behind you and scorn in the one ahead.*

A man's car once stalled in heavy Friday-evening traffic just as the light turned green. All his efforts to start the engine failed. A chorus of honking rose from the cars behind him.

Feeling just as frustrated as those other drivers eager to get home or to their weekend destinations, he finally got out of his car and walked back to the first driver and said, "I'm sorry, but I can't seem to get my car started. If you'll go up there and give it a try, I'll stay here and blow your horn for you."

The person who is chronically impatient rarely makes another person go faster or arrive earlier. Rather, the effects are nearly always negative—to others as well as to the impatient person. Accidents occur more frequently in haste. Ulcers, headaches, and other health problems develop more quickly. And relationships can become more readily strained.

As an antidote for impatience, try giving yourself "ten more minutes." Get up ten minutes earlier every morning, leave ten minutes earlier, arrive ten minutes ahead of schedule, and so forth. You'll likely arrive at the end of the day feeling much more relaxed.

The end of the matter is better than its beginning, and patience is better than pride. Do not be quickly provoked in your spirit, for anger resides in the lap of fools.
ECCLESIASTES 7:8,9 (NIV)

Thomas Edison, who held 1,093 patents for his inventions—which include the electric light bulb, phonograph, and motion-picture camera, sold the rights to many of his inventions to Western Union and other large companies to keep his workshop going. Over time, others made far more money from Edison's inventions than he did, but this didn't seem to bother him a great deal. He once said, "I don't care so much about making my fortune as I do for getting ahead of the other fellow." Edison's greatest desire was to be both the first

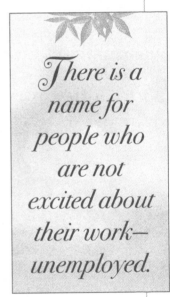

There is a name for people who are not excited about their work—unemployed.

and the best in his field, to outinvent everybody he could. He worked tirelessly, with joy.

Edison eventually established Menlo Park, the world's first factory for the making of nothing but inventions. It was a forerunner of the private research laboratories now maintained by many large companies. At Menlo Park, Edison promised to turn out "a minor invention every ten days and a big thing every six months or so." At one point, he was working on forty-seven things at once.

Other inventors may have been richer than Edison, but virtually no inventor has ever become more enthusiastic or more successful. For him, enthusiasm and employment were inextricably bound together!

And whatsoever ye do, do it heartily,
as to the Lord, and not unto men.
COLOSSIANS 3:23

> *A person's true character is revealed by what he does when no one is watching.*

Ted Engstrom tells the following story in his book titled *Integrity:*

"For Coach Cleveland Stroud and the Bulldogs of Rockdale County High School (Conyers, Georgia), it was their championship season: 21 wins and 5 losses on the way to the Georgia boy's basketball tournament last March, then a dramatic come-from-behind victory in the state finals.

"But now the new glass trophy case outside the highschool gymnasium is bare. Earlier this month the Georgia High School Association deprived Rockdale County of the championship after school officials said that a player who was scholastically ineligible had played

45 seconds in the first of the school's postseason games.

" 'We didn't know he was ineligible at the time; we didn't know it until a few weeks ago,' Mr. Stroud said. 'Some people have said we should have just kept quiet about it, that it was just 45 seconds and the player wasn't an impact player. But you've got to do what's honest and right and what the rules say. I told my team that people forget the scores of basketball games; they don't ever forget what you're made of.'"

Obey them not only to win their favor
when their eye is on you, but like slaves of
Christ, doing the will of God from your heart.
EPHESIANS 6:6 (NIV)

A man once went to his attorney and made this request: "I am going into a business deal with a man I do not trust. I want you to frame an airtight contract that he can't break, and which will protect me from any sort of mischief he may have on his mind."

The attorney replied: "Frankly, there's no group of words in the English language that can take the place of plain honesty between men. There's nothing that can be put into a contract that will *fully* protect either of you if one of you *plans* to deceive the other."

It's better to die with a good name than to live with a bad one.

Your name is tied to your character. If your character is bad, so will be your name. You are wise to establish a reputation for having a good name, a reputation for being honest, trustworthy, and steadfast. Your name will not only follow you all the days of your life but all the days of your children's lives as well.

Before entering into a business deal or employment relationship, ask yourself:

1.   How has this person treated others? Talk to his former associates, clients, vendors, and former employees.

2.   How does this person talk about business? Does he brag about destroying others, or winning by shrewdness? If so, you are likely dealing with a scheming person who attempts to "use" people.

Work with those who have sterling reputations. Your own reputation is less likely to become tarnished.

A good name is better than precious ointment.
ECCLESIASTES 7:1

> *"No"* is one of the few
> words that can never
> be misunderstood.

Although taken captive as children, Hananiah, Mishael, and Azariah were so wise that as adults, they were put over the affairs of Babylon province. Then the king they served built a gold image some 100 feet high and placed it in their province. He invited the empire's leaders to a dedication of the image and gave a command that when a tribute of music was sounded, all should fall and worship the golden image. Whoever didn't do so would be thrown into a giant furnace.

The music played, and all fell on their faces . . . except Hananiah, Mishael, and Azariah. They were Jews, and had been taught from earliest memory to never worship a graven image. Word of their refusal quickly came to the king, and in a rage, the king summoned them. The three leaders didn't hesitate in saying to the king, "We will not serve your gods, nor worship the golden image" (Daniel 3:18).

Furious, the king had the three cast into the fire, only to find that they did *not* burn. They emerged unscorched! The "no" of these faithful men resulted in the king decreeing that no person in the land speak anything against their God. And Hananiah, Mishael, and Azariah—whom the king called Shadrach, Meshach, and Abed-nego—were promoted.

If your answer is "no" than make it mean something. When you stand by your word God will stand by you.

But let your statement be
"yes, yes" or "no, no" . . . .
MATTHEW 5:37 (NASB)

The story is told of a lazy boy who went with his mother and aunt on a blueberry-picking hike into the woods. He carried the smallest pail possible. While the others worked hard at picking berries, he lolled about, chasing a butterfly and playing hide and seek with a squirrel. Soon it was approaching time to leave. In a panic, he filled his pail mostly with moss and then topped it off with a thin layer of berries, so that the pail looked full of berries. His mother and aunt commended him highly for his effort.

> Too many churchgoers are singing "Standing on the Promises" when all they are doing is sitting on the premises.

The next morning his mother baked pies, and she made a special "saucer-sized" pie just for the boy. He could hardly wait for it to cool. Blueberry was his favorite! He could see the plump berries oozing through a slit in the crust, and his mouth watered in anticipation. However, as he sunk his fork into the flaky crust, he found . . . mostly moss!

Many people *want* to experience the fullness of God's promises in their lives, but they are unwilling to do the work that goes along with most of the Bible's promises. Most of God's promises are if-then statements . . . if we do one thing, God will do another. Our part nearly always comes first!

That ye be not slothful, but followers
of them who through faith and
patience inherit the promises.
HEBREWS 6:12

Some people complain because God puts thorns on roses, while others praise Him for putting roses among thorns.

The pessimist will see a glass filled to the half-way mark with water as being half empty, the optimist as being half full. And the optimistically *creative* person will see it as a vase for a rosebud, the optimistic *pragmatist* as a means of quenching thirst, the optimistic *priest* as water to bless for baptism!

Consider the benefits of choosing the optimistic route as described in this poem:

Two frogs fell into a deep cream bowl,
One was an optimistic soul;
But the other took the gloomy view,
"I shall drown," he cried " and so will you."
So with a last despairing cry,
He closed his eyes and said, "Good-bye."
But the other frog, with a merry grin

Said, "I can't get out, but I won't give in!"
I'll swim around till my strength is spent.
For having tried, I'll die content."
Bravely he swam until it would seem
His struggles began to churn the cream.
On the top of the butter at last he stopped
And out of the bowl he happily hopped.
What is the moral? It's easily found.
If you can't get out—keep swimming around!

Finally, brethren, whatsoever things
are true, whatsoever things are honest,
whatsoever things are just, whatsoever
things are pure, whatsoever things are
lovely, whatsoever things are of good report;
if there be any virtue, and if there be
any praise, think on these things.

PHILIPPIANS 4:8

The importance of the first few years of a child's life cannot be overestimated. It is during those years that the foundation is laid for a child's language ability, ethics, morality, and value systems. In his book, *All Men Are Brothers,* Mahatma Gandhi said this about the instilling of values in very early childhood: "I am convinced that for the proper upbringing of children the parents ought to have a general knowledge of he care and nursing of babies . . . . We labour under a sort of superstition that the child has nothing to learn during the first five years of its life. On the contrary, the fact is that the child never learns in after life what it does in its first five years. The education of the child begins with conception."

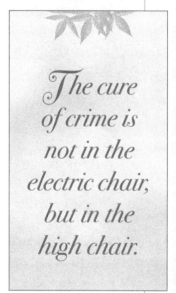

The cure of crime is not in the electric chair, but in the high chair.

The famous psychoanalyst Sigmund Freud agreed. A Viennese woman once asked him, "How early should I begin the education of my child?"

Freud replied with a question of his own, "When will the child be born?"

"Born?" the woman asked. "Why, he is already five years old!"

"My goodness woman," Freud cried, "don't stand there talking to me—hurry home! You have already wasted the best five years!"

Train up a child in the way
he should go; and when he is old,
he will not depart from it.
PROVERBS 22:6

> *The bridge you burn now may be the one you later have to cross.*

When Abraham Lincoln was campaigning for the presidency, one of his archenemies was Edwin McMasters Stanton. Stanton hated Lincoln, and used every ounce of his energy to degrade Lincoln in the eyes of the public, often using the bitterest diatribes in an attempt to embarrass him.

In the process of choosing his cabinet after his election, Lincoln selected various members and then faced a decision about the important post of Secretary of War. He chose Stanton! The president's inner circle erupted in an uproar when they heard his choice. Numerous advisors came to Lincoln saying, "Mr. President, you are making a mistake. Are you familiar with all the ugly things he has said about you? He is your enemy. He will sabotage your programs."

Lincoln replied, "Yes, I know Mr. Stanton. But . . . I find he is the best man for the job."

As Secretary of War, Stanton gave invaluable service to his nation and his president. After Lincoln was assassinated, many laudable statements were made about Abraham Lincoln, but the words of Stanton remain among the greatest. Standing near Lincoln's coffin, Stanton called Lincoln one of the greatest men who ever lived and said, "He now belongs to the ages."

If it be possible, as much as lieth
in you, live peaceably with all men.
Romans 12:18

In 1873, a Belgian Catholic priest named Joseph Damien De Veuster was sent to minister to lepers on the Hawaiian island of Molokai. He arrived in high spirits, hoping to build a friendship with each of the lepers. People shunned him, however, at every turn. He built a chapel, began worship services, poured his heart out to the lepers, but all seemed futile. No one responded to his ministry and after twelve years of struggling, Father Damien decided to leave. As he stood in dejection on the dock waiting to board the ship, he looked down at the hands he was wringing and noticed some mysterious white spots on them. Feeling some numbness, he knew immediately what was happening—he had contracted leprosy!

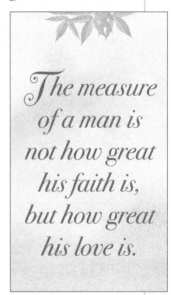

The measure of a man is not how great his faith is, but how great his love is.

Father Damien returned to the leper colony and to his work. Word spread quickly and within hours, hundreds gathered outside his hut, fully identifying with his plight. A bigger surprise came the following Sunday. When he arrived at the chapel, he found it full! Father Damien began to preach from the empathy of love rather than the distance of theology and ideas, and his ministry became enormously successful.

Those who receive your love today will be much more interested in hearing about your faith tomorrow.

And now these three remain: faith, hope and love. But the greatest of these is love.
1 CORINTHIANS 13:13 (NIV)

Real friends are those who, when you've made a fool of yourself, don't feel you've done a permanent job.

One of the most noble friendships in literature is that which Melanie has with Scarlett O'Hara in Margaret Mitchell's classic, *Gone with the Wind*. Melanie is characterized as a woman who "always saw the best in everyone and remarked kindly upon it." Even when Scarlett tries to confess her shameful behavior toward Ashley, Melanie's husband, Melanie says, "Darling, I don't want any explanation . . . . Do you think I could remember you walking in a furrow behind that Yankee's horse almost barefooted and with your hands blistered—just so the baby and I could have something to eat—and then believe such dreadful things about you? I don't want to hear a word."

Melanie's refusal to believe ill of Scarlett leads Scarlett to passionately desire to "keep Melanie's high opinion. She only knew that she did not care what the world thought of her or what Ashley or Rhett thought of her, but Melanie must not think her other than she had always thought her." It is as Melanie lays dying that Scarlett faces her deep need for Melanie's pure and generous friendship: "Panic clutching at her heart, she knew that Melanie had been her sword and her shield, her comfort and her strength." In two words, Melanie had been her *true friend*.

*Beareth all things, believeth all
things, hopeth all things, endureth
all things. Charity never faileth.*
1 CORINTHIANS 13:7,8

Newspaper columnist and minister George Crane tells of a wife who came to his office full of hatred toward her husband. Fully intending to divorce her husband, she said, "Before I divorce him, I want to hurt him as much as he has me."

Crane advised that she go home and act as if she really loved her husband. "Tell him how much he means to you," he said. "Praise him for every decent trait. Go out of your way to be as kind, considerate, and generous as possible. Spare no efforts to please him . . . then drop the bomb . . . . That will really hurt him."

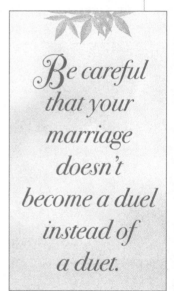

Be careful that your marriage doesn't become a duel instead of a duet.

The woman exclaimed, "Beautiful!" And she did as he had suggested . . . with enthusiasm, acting "as if" she loved him. Two months later she returned to Crane, who asked, "Are you ready now to go through with the divorce?"

"Divorce!" she said. "Never! I discovered I really do love him!"

Actions can change feelings. Motion can result in emotion. Love is established not so much by fervent promise as by often-repeated deeds.

Let us therefore follow after the things which make for peace, and things wherewith one may edify another.
ROMANS 14:19

> *The mighty oak was once a
> little nut that stood its ground.*

In the 1960s, drug companies were present-ing nearly 700 applications a year to the Federal Drug Administration (FDA) for new medicines. The beleaguered New Drug Section only had sixty days to review each drug before giving approval or requesting more data.

A few months after Dr. Frances Kelsey joined the FDA, an established pharmaceutical firm in Ohio applied for a license to market a new drug, Kevadon. In liquid form, the drug seemed to relieve nausea in early pregnancy. It was given to millions of expectant women, mostly in Europe, Asia, and Africa. Although scientific studies revealed harmful side effects, the pharmaceutical firm printed 66,957 leaflets declaring its safety. The company exerted great pressure on Dr. Kelsey to give permission for labels to be printed, in anticipation of the drug's approval.

Dr. Kelsey reviewed the data and said no. Through several rounds of applications, she continued to find the data "unsatisfactory." After a fourteen-month struggle, the company humbly withdrew its application. "Kevadon" was thalidomide, and by that name, the horror of thalidomide deformities was becoming well publicized! One firm "no" decision by Dr. Kelsey spared untold agony in the United States.

Sometimes standing your ground on something may not seem that important but in time you may see the "big" picture.

A man shall not be established by wickedness: but the root of the righteous shall not be moved.

PROVERBS 12:3

Jane was only seven years old when she visited a shabby street in a nearby town, and seeing ragged children there, announced that she wanted to build a big house so poor children would have a place to play. As a young adult, Jane and a friend, Ellen Starr, visited Toynbee Hall in London, where they saw educated people helping the poor by living among them. She and Ellen returned to the slums of Chicago, restored the old Hull mansion, and moved in! There they cared for children of working mothers, and held sewing and cooking classes. Older boys and girls had clubs at the mansion. An art gallery, playground, and public music, reading, and craft rooms were created in the mansion. Her childhood dream came true!

The secret of achievement is to not let what you're doing get to you before you get to it.

Jane fought against child labor laws, and campaigned for adult education, day nurseries, better housing, and women's suffrage. She eventually was awarded an honorary degree from Yale, and was called "America's most useful citizen" by President Theodore Roosevelt, and was given the Nobel Prize for Peace.

No matter how famous she became, however, Jane Addams remained a resident of Hull House. She died a resident of Halsted Street in the heart of the slum she had come to call home.

Commit thy works unto the Lord,
and thy thoughs shall be established.
PROVERBS 16:3

GLDB

> *Most people wish to serve God—but only in an advisory capacity.*

An old poem tells of a woman who was walking through a meadow one day. As she strolled along, meditating on nature, she came upon a field of golden pumpkins. In the corner of the field stood a majestic, huge oak tree.

The woman sat under the oak tree and began musing about the strange twists in nature—why tiny acorns grew on huge branches and huge pumpkins on tiny vines. She thought, *God blundered with creation! He should have put the small acorns on the tiny vines and the large pumpkins on the huge branches.*

Before long, the woman dozed off in the warmth of the late autumn sunshine. She was awakened when a tiny acorn bounced off her nose. Chuckling to herself, she amended her previous thinking, *Maybe God was right after all!*

In every situation, God knows far more about the people and circumstances involved than we can ever know. He alone sees the beginning from the ending. He alone knows how to create a Master Plan that provides for the good of *all* those who serve Him.

*Humble yourselves therefore
under the mighty hand of God,
that he may exalt you in due time.*
1 PETER 5:6

These lines from Dr. Arnot give an interesting description of a person's conscience: "A man may be saved from death by seeing the reflection of danger in a mirror, when the danger itself could not be directly seen. The executioner with his weapon is stealthily approaching through a corridor of a castle to the spot where the devoted invalid reclines. In his musings, the captive has turned his vacant eye towards a mirror on the wall; and the faithful witness reveals the impending stroke in time to secure the escape of the victim. It is thus that the mirror in a man's breast has become in a sense the man's savior, by revealing the wrath to come before its coming. Happy they who take the warning; happy they who turn and live!"

Conscience is God's built-in warning system. Be very happy when it hurts you. Be very worried when it doesn't.

It has been said that man's conscience was given to him after the Fall in the Garden of Eden. Man's desire to know good and evil had been granted. But God, in His mercy, gave man a means of telling good *from* evil. That mechanism, which He placed in man's heart was the conscience. Don't ignore the promptings of your conscience or let your conscience become calloused. It's more than a sixth sense. It's a beacon whose homing signal is Heaven.

And herein do I exercise myself,
to have always a conscience void of
offense toward God, and toward men.
ACTS 24:16

> *Most men forget God all day and ask Him to remember them at night.*

Many people revere Francis of Assisi, the thirteenth-century saint known for his very simple lifestyle and deep love of the poor. He founded the Franciscan order, restored numerous dilapidated Italian chapels, and helped countless needy people.

What most people don't know, however, is that Francis spent most of his life not in doing good works, but in prayer. St. Bonaventure wrote about him, "Whether walking or sitting, within doors or without, at toil or at leasure, he was so absorbed in prayer that he seemed to have devoted not only his whole heart and body, but also his whole heart and time." Francis regularly set aside hours throughout the day which he called "appointments with

God," and he never missed one, even though he had serious eye, stomach, spleen, and liver problems. On one occasion, as Francis traveled through the large town of Borgo on a donkey, people pressed in upon him from all sides to touch his garments. Francis was so absorbed in prayer that when he arrived at his destination some time later, he asked when they were going to get to Borgo!

No matter how busy we are, we must never become too busy to pray. It is our prayer life that gives lasting meaning to everything else we undertake.

Evening, and morning, and
at noon, will I pray, and cry aloud:
and he shall hear my voice.
PSALM 55:17

As legend has it, a just and good man went to Sodom one day, hoping to save the city from God's judgment. He tried to talk to first one individual and then the next, but nobody would engage in conversation with him.

Next, he tried carrying a picket sign that had "Repent" written on it in large letters. Nobody paid any attention to his sign after an initial glance.

If you don't stand for something you'll fall for anything!

Finally he began going from street to street and from marketplace to marketplace, shouting loudly, "Men and women, repent! What you are doing is wrong. It will kill you! It will destroy you!"

The people laughed at him, but still he went about shouting. One day, a person stopped him and said, "Stranger, can't you see that your shouting is useless?" The man replied, "Yes, I see that." The person then asked, "So, why do you continue?"

The man said, "When I arrived in this city, I was convinced that I could change them. Now I continue shouting because I don't want them to change me."

Speak out for those things that you believe to be true and good. If you remain silent, others may take your silence as agreement with their position—which may not be at all what you believe.

If you do not stand firm in your faith, you will not stand at all.
ISAIAH 7:9 (NIV)

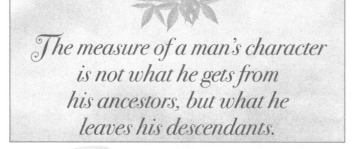

*The measure of a man's character
is not what he gets from
his ancestors, but what he
leaves his descendants.*

"If I can throw a single ray of light across the darkened pathway of another; if I can aid some soul to clearer sight of life and duty, and thus bless my brother; if I can wipe from any human cheek a tear, I shall not have lived my life in vain while here.

"If I can guide some erring one to truth, inspire within his heart a sense of duty; if I can plant within my soul of rosy youth a sense of right, a love of truth and beauty; if I can teach one man that God and heaven are near, I shall not have lived in vain while here.

"If from my mind I banish doubt and fear, and keep my life attuned to love and kindness; if I can scatter light and hope and cheer, and help remove the curse of mental blindness; if

I can make more joy, more hope, less pain, I shall not have lived and loved in vain.

"If by life's roadside I can plant a tree, beneath whose shade some wearied head may rest, though I may never share its beauty, I shall yet be truly blest—though no one knows my name, nor drops a flower upon my grave, I shall not have lived in vain while here."—*Anonymous*

A good man leaveth an inheritance to his children's children: and the wealth of the sinner is laid up for the just.

PROVERBS 13:22

Ida and David both wanted their sons to graduate from college. They knew their boys would have to pay their own way since David never made more than $150 a month. Still, they encouraged their sons to achieve all they could. Arthur, however, went directly from high school to a job. Edgar began studying law. When Dwight graduated, he didn't have a goal in mind, so he and Ed made a pact: Dwight would work two years while Ed studied, sending Ed as much as he could, and then they would reverse the arrangement. While working Dwight found an opportunity that appealed to him more than college—West Point.

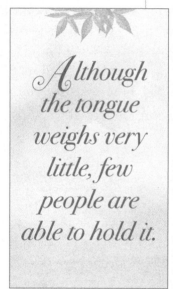

Although the tongue weighs very little, few people are able to hold it.

Both Ida and David were crushed by Dwight's decision. Ida was deeply convinced that soldiering was wicked. Still, all she ever said to him was, "It is your choice." David also remained silent, allowing his adult son full freedom to forge his own adult future. Yes, Ida and David wisely held their tongues—but they never withheld their applause, especially on the day their son, *General* Dwight Eisenhower, became President of the United States of America.

Refraining from giving advice may actually turn out to be the best gift you may ever give a person.

Even so the tongue is a little member,
and boasteth great things. Behold,
how great a matter a little fire kindleth!
JAMES 3:5

> *You should never let adversity get you down—except on your knees.*

A young soldier fighting in Italy during World War II managed to jump into a foxhole just ahead of a spray of bullets. He immediately attempted to deepen the hole for more protection. As he was frantically scraping at the dirt with his hands, he unearthed a silver crucifix, obviously left by a previous occupant of the foxhole. A moment later, a leaping figure landed beside him as shells screamed overhead. The soldier turned to see that his new companion was an army chaplain. Holding up the crucifix, the soldier cried, "Am I glad to see you! How do you work this thing?"

On a more serious note, Captain Eddie Rickenbacker wrote about his World War II experience. While flying on a special mission to the Pacific Islands, his plane crashed. He and his crew were lost at sea for twenty-one days before being rescued. He said, "In the beginning many of the men were atheists or agnostics, but at the end of the terrible ordeal each, in his own way, had discovered God. Each man found salvation and strength in prayer, and a community of feeling developed which created a liveliness of human fellowship and worship, and a sense of gentle peace."

Are you facing a problem today? Start the search for its solution with prayer.

Is any one of you in trouble?
He should pray . . . .
JAMES 5:13 (NIV)

Miss Jones, an elderly spinster, was the oldest resident of her Midwestern town on the day she died. In writing her obituary, the editor of the local paper became stumped after noting her age. Miss Jones had never spent a night in jail or been seen intoxicated on the streets. She also had never done anything noteworthy. While musing about what he might write, the editor went out for cofee and in the local café, he met the owner of the tombstone company, who was equally perplexed as to what to write about Miss Jones.

He who wants milk should not sit on a stool in the middle of the pasture expecting the cow to back up to him.

The editor turned to his office and assigned both the obituary and tombstone epitaph to the first reporter he saw, who happened to be the sports editor. If you pass through that little town, you'll find this on Miss Jones' tombstone:

Here lies the bones of Nancy Jones
For her life held no terrors.
She lived an old maid. She died an
     old maid.
No hits, no runs, no errors.

If we don't try, we don't do . . . if we don't do . . . we can't bless others. We each have a contribution to make to the lives of others. Give your best effort today. It's your best shot at scoring in the game of life.

He becometh poor that dealeth
with a slack hand: but the hand
of the diligent maketh rich.
PROVERBS 10:4

> *The best bridge between hope and despair is often a good night's sleep.*

When the call came from Steve Early, President Roosevelt's press secretary, Harry Truman responded immediately. He arrived only minutes later at the front door of the White House, stopping only to pick up his hat, but leaving his Secret Service escort behind. He was ushered directly to Mrs. Roosevelt's suite, where the First Lady rose to greet him, then put her arm around his shoulder and said, "The President is dead."

This was the first inkling that Truman had of the seriousness of Franklin Roosevelt's condition. He asked if he could do anything for Mrs. Roosevelt and the family, and she replied by asking him if there was anything they could do for him. Truman then went to the Oval Office and called his wife Bess, who relayed to daughter Margaret what had happened. They both came quickly to the White House and by seven o'clock that evening, Harry Truman had been sworn into office. The family went home and as was later noted in Truman's diary, "[The neighbors] gave us something to eat. I had not had anything to eat since noon. I went to bed, went to sleep, and did not worry any more." The next morning, he went to the Oval Office and began to master the job he always liked to say was the greatest in the world.

It is vain for you to rise up early, to
sit up late, to eat the bread of sorrows:
for so he giveth his beloved sleep.
PSALM 127:2

An old legend tells how a man once stumbled upon a great red barn after wandering for days in a dark, overgrown forest. Seeking refuge from the howling winds of a storm that seemed to rage perpetually in the forest, he let his eyes grow accustomed to the dark and then, to his astonishment, he discovered that this was the barn where Satan kept his storehouse of seeds to be sown into human hearts. More curious than fearful, he lit a match and began to explore the piles and bins of seeds around him. He couldn't help but notice that the containers labeled "seeds of discouragement" far outnumbered any other type of seed.

It is good to remember that the tea kettle, although up to its neck in hot water, continues to sing.

Just as the man had drawn this conclusion, one of Satan's foremost demons arrived to pick up a fresh supply of seed. The man asked him why the great abundance of discouragement seeds. The demon laughed, "Because they are so effective and they take root so quickly!" The man then asked, "Do they grow everywhere?" At this the demon became sullen. He glared at the man and admitted in disgust, "No. They never seem to thrive in the heart of a grateful person."

Be thankful for what you have, today. And trust the Lord to take care of what you *don't* have.

Rejoice evermore. In every thing give thanks: for this is the will of God in Christ Jesus concerning you.
1 THESSALONIANS 5:16,18

> *It's good to be a Christian and know it, but it's better to be a Christian and show it!*

In *Les Misérables,* Victor Hugo tells of Jean Valjean, whose only crime was the theft of a loaf of bread to feed his sister's starving children. Valjean served nineteen years for this crime before being turned out penniless on the streets. Hardened and unable to find work as a former convict, Valjean finally makes his way to the home of a good old bishop, who gives him supper and a bed for the night. He serves Valjean using his best silver platters and candlesticks, which Valjean recognizes as being highly valuable.

Yielding to temptation, Valjean steals the bishop's silver plates and slips away from the bishop's home, but is soon caught and returned by watchful police. When shown the silver plates, the bishop says to the apprehending policeman, "Why, I gave them to him." And then turning to the thief Valjean, he adds, "And Jean, you forgot to take the candlesticks." A shocked and eternally grateful Valjean accepts the candlesticks as more than valuable silver pieces, but as expressions of love beyond measure. The bishop's act brought about a true repentance and changed life.

Who knows which person might be impacted by your act of kindness today? What seems little to you may be great in the eyes of a person in need of love.

> *By this shall all men know that*
> *ye are my disciples, if ye*
> *have love one to another.*
> JOHN 13:35

*I*n *Love and Duty,* Anne Purcell writes about seeing Major Jim Statler standing with her pastor outside his study after a Sunday service. She knew instantly that he was there with news about her husband, Ben, on active duty in Vietnam. As she feared, Jim gave her a chilling message: "He was on a helicopter that was shot down . . . he's missing in action."

Sorrow looks back.

Worry looks around.

Faith looks up.

Anne recalls, "Somewhere in the back of my mind, a little candle flame flickered. This tiny flame was the vestige of my faith." Days passed without a word. To her, being a MIA wife was like being in limbo. She found herself only able to pray one thing: "Help me, dear Father." She says, "I hung onto this important truth—that He would help me—and the flickering flame of my candle of faith began to grow." Then, one day, she noticed a white dove sitting in her yard. It was particularly beautiful, very still and quiet, and a highly uncommon sight in her neighborhood. She took it as a sign from God that He was, indeed, always near.

For five years, Anne Purcell clung to the fact that God was near. Little did she know that during those years before she was reunited with her husband, he was whispering to her from a POW cell, "Anne, find solace and strength in the Lord."

Fixing our eyes on Jesus, the author and perfecter of faith, who for the joy set before Him endured the cross, despising the shame, and has sat down at the right hand of the throne of God.
HEBREWS 12:2 (NASB)

> *A man is never in worse company than when he flies into a rage and is beside himself.*

A little girl was once in a very bad mood. She took her frustration out on her younger brother, at first just teasing him, but eventually punching him, pulling his hair, and kicking him in the shins. The boy could take it all—and even dish back a few blows—until the kicking began. That hurt! And he went crying to his mother, complaining about what his sister had done.

The mother came to the little girl and said, "Mary, why have you let Satan put it into your heart to pull your brother's hair and kick his shins?"

The little girl thought it over for a moment and then answered, "Well, Mother, maybe

Satan did put it into my heart to pull Tommy's hair . . .but kicking his shins was my own idea."

All the evil in the world doesn't come from direct satanic involvement. Much of it comes from the heart of man. What we do with our anger, feelings of hatred, and frustrations is subject to our *will*. We can choose how we will respond to stress, or to the behavior of others. Our challenge is to *govern* our emotions; otherwise, they will rule in tyranny over us.

He that is soon angry dealeth foolishly . . .
PROVERBS 14:17

In Thornton Wilder's play *The Skin of Our Teeth,* the character Mrs. Antrobus says to her husband, "I didn't marry you because you were perfect . . . I married you because you gave me a promise."

She then takes off her ring and looks at it, saying, "That promise made up for your faults and the promise I gave you made up for mine. Two imperfect people got married, and it was the promise that made the marriage."

> *Success in marriage is more than finding the right person. It's becoming the right person.*

In every marriage, no matter how well the two people know one another, great mysteries remain! Very often, each person comes to the marriage

- not fully knowing himself or herself,

- not fully knowing about life, and

- not fully knowing about his or her spouse.

What is unknown is far greater than what is known!

Becoming a faithful, loving spouse not only takes courage and faith, but patience and a desire to keep learning and growing. Better than the question, "What kind of spouse do I desire to have?" is the question, "What kind of spouse do I aspire to be?"

But thou, O man of God, flee these things; and follow after righteousness, godliness, faith, love, patience, meekness.
1 TIMOTHY 6:11

> *Failure in people is caused more by lack of determination than lack in talent.*

In 1982, internal-medicine resident Barry Marshall was frustrated that there was no cure for his patients with ulcers. Then, while studying a stomach biopsy, he saw organisms resembling *Campylobacter* bacteria, first identified by his hospital's pathologist, Dr. J. Robbin Warren. Warren and Marshall studied 100 ulcer patients for a year, and found the bacteria in 87 percent of the cases. Leading specialists, however, insisted the bacteria developed *after* the specimens were removed. For decades, clinical researchers had concluded that ulcers were based on weak stomach linings. Marshall's bacterial theory was snubbed.

Warren and Marshall cultured the bacteria for observation and found that a combination of bismuth and antibiotics destroyed it. Again, their report was met with skepticism. Marshall reported study after study. Still, doctors refused to conduct clinical trials. Finally, trials began in 1986, four years after Marshall's initial findings. These studies confirmed both Marshall's bacterial theory and his treatment methods.

Because a young internist "wouldn't accept no" from the medical community, the vast majority of ulcers, and some stomach cancers, can now be treated successfully!

*And let us not be weary in
well doing: for in due season
we shall reap, if we faint not.*
GALATIANS 6:9

Fulton Oursler told a story of an old nurse who was born a slave on the eastern shore of Maryland. She had not only attended Fulton's birth, but that of his mother. He credits her for teaching him the greatest lesson he ever learned about giving thanks and finding contentment. Recalls Oursler:

I remember her as she sat at the kitchen table in our house; the hard, old, brown hands folded across her starched apron, the glistening eyes, and the husky old whispering voice, saying, "Much obliged, Lord, for my vittles."

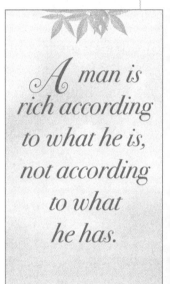

A man is rich according to what he is, not according to what he has.

"Anna," I asked, "what's a vittle?"

"It's what I've got to eat and drink—that's vittles," the old nurse replied.

"But you'd get your vittles whether you thanked the Lord or not."

"Sure," said Anna, "but it makes everything taste better to be thankful."

Poverty is not a state of the pocketbook for many people, but a state of mind. Do you think of yourself as being rich or poor today? What is it that you truly count as "wealth" in your life? If you list things that are *not* material in nature, you are likely very wealthy indeed!

There is that maketh himself rich,
yet hath nothing: there is that maketh
himself poor, yet hath great riches.
PROVERBS 13:7

> *Life can only be understood by looking backward, but it must be lived by looking forward.*

On New Year's day, 1929, Georgia Tech played the University of California in the Rose Bowl. In the first half, Roy Riegels recovered a fumble for California, but he became confused about direction and ran the wrong way. One of his teammates tackled him just yards before he scored for the opposing team. When California tried to punt, Tech blocked the kick and scored a safety, which became the winning margin.

During halftime, the California players sat quietly, waiting to hear what the coach had to say. He was uncharacteristically quiet. Riegels put his blanket around his shoulders, stayed in a corner, put his face in his hands, and cried like a baby. Three minutes before playing time, Coach Price looked at the team and said simply, "Men, the same team that played the first half will start the second."

The players filed on the field, but Riegels did not budge. "Roy, didn't you hear me?" the coach asked.

Riegels responded, "I couldn't face the crowd in the stadium to save my life." Coach Price put his hand on Roy's shoulder and said, "Roy, get up and go on back; the game is only half over." Tech men to this day will tell you they have never seen a man play football as Roy Riegels played that second half.

*And Jesus said unto him, "No man,
having put his hand to the plow, and
looking back, is fit for the kingdom of God."*
LUKE 9:62

Perhaps more than any other leader in the twentieth century, Winston Churchill rallied a nation to believe in what it *could* do. His speeches during World War II not only express resolution, but a profound peace of mind and a feeling of "rightness." Here are some of his words to England and the world:

"You ask what is our policy? I will say: It is to wage war, by sea, land, and air, with all our might and all the strength that God can give us . . . . You ask, What is our aim? I can answer in one word: Victory . . . at all costs, victory in spite of all terror, victory however long and hard the road may be; for without victory there is no survival . . . .

Success comes in cans; failure comes in can'ts.

We shall go on to the end, we shall fight in France, we shall fight on the seas and oceans, we shall fight with growing confidence and growing strength in the air, we shall defend our island, whatever the cost may be; we shall fight on the beaches, we shall fight on the landing grounds, we shall fight in the fields and in the streets, we shall fight in the hills; we shall never surrender."

What wonderful words to adapt to any fight against evil!

I can do all things through
Christ which strengtheneth me.
PHILIPPIANS 4:13

GLDB

> *Sometimes we are so busy adding up our troubles that we forget to count our blessings.*

For decades, Grandpa had been stubborn and crabby. His wife, children, and grandchildren seemed to be able to do nothing that pleased him. As far as he was concerned, life was filled with nothing but bad times and big troubles. Eventually, his family expected only a gruff growl from Grandpa.

Then overnight, Grandpa changed. Gentleness and optimism marked his new personality. Positive words and compliments poured from his lips. He could even be heard giving joyful praise to the Lord. One of the family members noted, "I think maybe "Grandpa found religion." Another replied, "Maybe so, but maybe it's something else. I'm going to ask him what has happened." The young man went to his grandfather and said, "Gramps, what has caused you to change so suddenly?"

"Well, son," the old man replied, "I've been striving in the face of incredible problems all my life—and for what? The hope of a contented *mind*. It's done no good, nope, not one bit, so . . . I've decided to be contented without it."

Never start counting your troubles until you've counted at least a hundred of your blessings. By that time, you probably won't think you have troubles!

I will remember the works of the Lord:
surely I will remember thy wonders
of old. I will meditate also of all
thy work, and talk of thy doings.
PSALM 77:11,12

Most people know that Thomas Edison conducted countless experiments with countless kinds of materials in search for an effective filament to use in carbon incandescent lamps. As each fiber failed, he would toss it out the window. Ultimately, the pile of failures reached to the second story of his house.

One day in 1879, some thirteen months after his first failure, he succeeded in finding a filament that would stand the stress of electric current. Here's how: Edison casually picked up a bit of lampblack, mixed it with tar, rolled it into a thin thread, and thought, *Why not try a carbonized carbon fiber?* He worked for five hours to make a fiber but it broke in two before he removed the mold. He used two spools of cotton thread before a perfect strand

Falling down doesn't make you a failure, but staying down does.

emerged, only to be ruined when he tried to place it in a glass tube. He continued without sleep for two days and nights before he managed to slip one of the carbonized threads into a vacuum-sealed bulb. Turning on the current, he saw the glow of electric light that we now take for granted.

A failure doesn't need to mark the end. It can be one step closer to the success you desire!

*For a just man falleth seven times,
and riseth up again . . . .*
PROVERBS 24:16

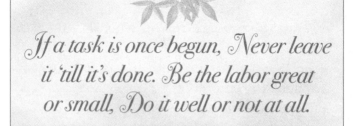

If a task is once begun, Never leave it 'till it's done. Be the labor great or small, Do it well or not at all.

The order from the head teacher was abrupt: "The classroom needs sweeping. Take the broom and sweep it."

Young Booker T. Washington knew that this was his chance. He swept the room three times, and then dusted the furniture four times. When the head teacher came back to evaluate his work, she inspected the floor closely and then used her handkerchief to rub the woodwork around the walls, the table, and the students' benches. When she could not find one speck of dust anywhere in the room, she said quietly, "I guess you will do to enter this institution."

Cleaning a classroom was nothing less than Booker T. Washington's entrance examination to Hampton Institute in Virginia. In later years, he would recall this as the turning point in his life. He wrote in his autobiography, *Up From Slavery*, "I have passed several examinations since then, but I have always felt that this was the best one I ever passed."

Slacking off, goofing off, and dozing off rarely open doors of opportunity. Those doors are opened best by a consistently excellent effort. Give the world an effort of that caliber today!

I have glorified thee on the earth;
I have finished the work
which thou gavest me to do.
JOHN 17:4

How many times have we said, or heard others say, "Manãna. I'll do it tomorrow." Sometimes people put off doing today what they know or want to do because they don't think they know enough or can perform well enough. The fact is, there is no "magic age" at which excellence emerges or quality surfaces.

Time is more valuable than money because time is irreplaceable.

Thomas Jefferson was 33 when he drafted the Declaration of Independence. Benjamin Franklin was 26 when he wrote *Poor Richard's Almanac*. Charles Dickens was 24 when he began his *Pickwick Papers* and 25 when he wrote *Oliver Twist*. Isaac Newton was 24 when he formulated the law of gravitation.

A second danger is to think that creativity and invention belong to the young. This is equally untrue! Emmanuel Kant wrote his finest philosophical works at age 74. Verdi at 80 produced *Falstaff* and at 85, *Ave Maria*. Goethe was 80 when he completed *Faust*. Tennyson was 80 when he wrote *Crossing the Bar* and Michelangelo completed his greatest work at 87. At 90, Justice Holmes was still writing brilliant Supreme Court opinions.

Seize the day! Redeem the "now" moments of your life. The moment you wait for may never arrive. The moment once past will never return.

Redeeming the time,
because the days are evil.
EPHESIANS 5:16

GLDB

> *The best way to forget your own problems is to help someone solve his.*

Sadhu Sundar Singh and a companion were traveling through a pass high in the Himalayan Mountains when they came across a body lying in the snow. They checked for vital signs and discovered the man still alive, but barely so. Sundar Singh prepared to stop and help this unfortunate traveler, but his companion objected, saying, "We shall lose our lives if we burden ourselves with him." Sundar Singh, however, could not think of leaving the man to die in the snow without an attempted rescue on his part. His companion quickly bade him farewell and walked on.

Sundar Singh lifted the poor traveler on his back. With great exertion on his part—made even greater by the high altitude and snowy conditions—he carried the man onward. As he walked, the heat cast off by his body began to warm the frozen man. He revived and soon, both were walking together side by side, each holding the other up, and in turn, each giving body heat to the other. Before long they came upon yet another traveler's body lying in the snow. Upon closer inspection, they discovered him to be dead, frozen by the cold.

He was Sundar Singh's original traveling companion.

Don't forget, by reaching out to help others you usually forget your own problems.

Look not every man on his own things,
but every man also on the things of others.
PHILIPPIANS 2:4

A boy once said to God, "I've been thinking, and I know what I want when I become a man." He proceeded to give God his list: to live in a big house with two Saint Bernards and a garden . . . marry a blue-eyed, tall, beautiful woman . . . have three sons—one who will be a senator, one a scientist, and one a quarterback. He also wanted to be an adventurer who climbed tall mountains . . . and to drive a red Ferrari.

God can heal a broken heart, but he has to have all the pieces.

As it turned out, the boy hurt his knee one day while playing football. He no longer could climb trees, much less mountains. He married a beautiful and kind woman, who was short with brown eyes. Because of his business, he lived in a city apartment, took cabs, and rode subways. He had three loving daughters, and they adopted a fluffy cat. One daughter became a nurse, another an artist, and the third a music teacher.

One morning the man awoke and remembered his boyhood dream. He became extremely depressed, so depressed that he became very ill. Close to death from a broken heart, he called out to God, "Remember when I was a boy and told You all the things I wanted? Why didn't You give me those things?"

"I could have," said God," but I wanted to make you happy."

Remember, God wants the best for us. Trust Him with your whole heart—He's the original heart surgeon.

My son, give me thine heart.
PROVERBS 23:26

> *Authority makes
> some people grow—
> and others just swell.*

Everybody knows of Isaac Newton's famed encounter with a falling apple, and how Newton introduced the laws of gravity and revolutionized astronomical studies. But few know that if it weren't for Edmund Halley, the world may never have heard of Newton. Halley was the one who challenged Newton to think through his original theories. He corrected Newton's mathematical errors and prepared geometrical figures to support his discoveries. It was Halley who coaxed the hesitant Newton to write his great work, *Mathematical Principles of Natural Philosophy.* And it was Halley who edited and supervised its publication, financing its printing even though Newton was wealthier and could better afford the cost.

Historians have called Halley's relationship with Newton one of the most selfless examples in science. Newton began almost immediately to reap the rewards of prominence; Halley received little credit. He did use the principles Newton developed to predict the orbit and return of a comet that would later bear his name, but since Halley's Comet only returns every 76 years, few hear his name. Still, Halley didn't care who received credit as long as the cause of science was advanced. He was content to live without fame.

Sometimes just the reward of *what* we are doing far outweighs the recognition we often think we need to have.

But he that is greatest among you shall be your servant. And whosoever shall exalt himself shall be abased; and he that shall humble himself shall be exalted.
MATTHEW 23:11,12

Jenny Lind was known as "The Swedish Nightingale" during her very successful career as an operatic singer. She became one of the wealthiest artists of her time, yet she left the stage at a time when she was singing her best. And, she never returned to it.

Countless people speculated as to the reason for her leaving, and most people wondered how she could give up so much applause, fame, and money. For her part, she seemed content to live in privacy in a home by the sea.

Be more concerned with what God thinks about you than what people think about you.

One day a friend found her on the sea sands, her Bible on her knees, looking out into the glorious glow of a sunset. As they talked, the friend asked, "Madame Goldschmidt, how is it that you came to abandon the stage at the height of your success?"

She answered quietly, "When every day made me think less of this (laying a finger on her Bible) and nothing at all of that (pointing to the sunset), what else could I do?"

The world may never understand your decision to follow God's ways. But then, perhaps God cannot understand a decision to pursue what the world offers.

Then Peter and the other apostles answered and said, "We ought to obey God rather than man."

ACTS 5:29

> *The trouble with the guy who talks too fast is that he often says something he hasn't thought of yet.*

Tom Kelly managed the Minnesota Twins to a World Series title in 1987, his first full season as their manager—and then managed them to their second world championship in 1991. Yet to watch him at work, critics have wondered if his vital signs have been stolen. Asked one sports writer, "How has T.K. *managed* all this, while lowering his blood pressure to the equivalent of the water pressure in your first apartment? He doesn't chew on fingernails or Rolaids or tobacco or his players. How?"

One of Kelly's trademarks is that he is a man of few words. He enjoys throwing during batting practice every day, in part because he believes that every minute he is throwing, he doesn't have to speak to the media. "I'm not really intelligent," T.K. claims. "I have a year and a half of college. But I have enough common sense to realize that I'm not intelligent. I realize that if I keep talking, I'll eventually say something dumb. So I don't give myself a lot of opportunities to open my mouth and stick my foot in it."

Tom Kelly is far from dumb. So is any person who is smart enough to limit what he says.

Be not rash with thy mouth, and let not thine heart be hasty to utter any thing before God: for God is in heaven, and thou, upon earth: therefore let thy words be few.
ECCLESIASTES 5:2

A woman in a fancy luxury car waited patiently in a crowded mall lot for a parking place to open up. She drove up and down between the rows until finally she saw a man with a load of packages head for his car. She followed him and parked behind him, waiting while he opened his trunk and loaded it. Finally he got into his car and backed out. Just as she was preparing to pull forward into the space, a young man in a little sports car—coming from the opposite direction—turned in front of her, zipped into the space, got

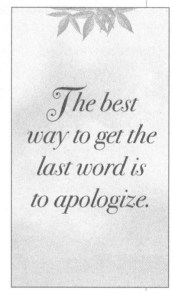

The best way to get the last word is to apologize.

out of his car, and started walking away. The woman was livid. She shouted from her big luxury car, "Hey, young man! I was waiting for that parking place."

The teenager responded, "Sorry, lady, but that's how it is when you're young and quick." She instantly put her car into gear, floorboarded it, and crashed into the sports car, crushing its right rear fender. Now it was the young man's turn to jump up and down, shouting, "What are you doing?" The woman in the luxury car calmly responded, "Well, son, that's how it is when you're old and rich."

Most of the world's problems and conflicts could probably be resolved if, instead of retaliation and revenge, apologies were made all around.

*If you have been trapped by what you said,
ensnared by the words of your mouth,
then do this, my son, to free yourself, since
you have fallen into your neighbor's
hands: Go and humble yourself;
press your plea with your neighbor!*
PROVERBS 6:2,3 (NIV)

> *The train of failure usually runs on the track of laziness.*

Success in business is often closely associated with a person's courage and ability to recover from his or her most recent failure!

In 1928,, a 33-year-old man by the name of Paul Galvin, found himself staring at failure . . . again. He had failed in business twice at this point, his competitors having forced him to fold his latest venture in the storage-battery business. Convinced, however, that he still had a marketable idea, Galvin attended the auction of his own business. With $750 he had managed to raise, he bought back the battery eliminator portion of the inventory. With it, he built a new company . . . one in which he succeeded . . . one from which he eventually retired . . . one that became a household word:

Motorola. Upon retirement, Galvin advised others: "Do not fear mistakes. You will know failure—continue to reach out."

A failure isn't truly a failure until you quit trying. If a venture begins to slow down, try speeding up your efforts. Consider the child who allows a bicycle to slow to a halt. Eventually the bicycle wobbles to the point where the child falls off. The key to turning around the crash? Faster peddling! The same holds true for many an enterprise.

By much slothfulness the building decayeth; and through idleness of the hands the house droppeth through.
ECCLESIASTES 10:18

One day the Pahouins brought a giant native in chains to Albert Schweitzer's hospital. In a fit of madness, N'Tschambi had killed a woman. Reaching down to help the man to the landing, Schweitzer saw fear and sadness in his face. When others refused his order to remove the man's chains, he did it himself. He then explained sedatives to N'Tschambi, and the fearful man gratefully accepted them. That night he slept for the first time without nightmares.

When confronted with a Goliath-sized problem, which way do you respond: "He's too big to hit," or like David, "He's too big to miss?"

N'Tschambi became a model patient and soon Schweitzer gave him periods of freedom outside his room, to which he often returned voluntarily if he became agitated. Still, any task he was given, he tackled with a fierce energy that frightened the staff. One day Schweitzer gave him an axe and asked him to help him make a clearing. N'Tschambi drew back in alarm, stating he was afraid to touch the axe for fear of what he might do with it. Schweitzer replied, "If I'm not afraid, why should you be?" The two then went into the jungle as the entire hospital watched. Hours later, they returned, N'Tschambi's big body dripping with sweat but a radiant smile on his lips. The giant inside him had been felled by kindness and the faith another human being had put in him!

. . . The LORD that delivered me out of the paw of the lion, and out of the paw of the bear, he will deliver me out of the hand of this Philistine.

1 SAMUEL 17:37

GLDB

> *Forget yourself for others and others will not forget you!*

Reporters and city officials gathered at a Chicago railroad station one afternoon in 1953. The person they were meeting was the 1952 Nobel Peace Prize winner. A few minutes after the train came to a stop, a giant of a man—six-feet-four—with bushy hair and a large moustache stepped from the train. Cameras flashed. City officials approached him with hands outstretched. Various ones began telling him how honored they were to meet him.

The man politely thanked them and then, looking over their heads, he asked if he could be excused for a moment. He quickly walked through the crowd until he reached the side of an elderly black woman who was struggling with two large suitcases. He picked up the bags and with a smile, escorted the woman to a bus. After helping her aboard, he wished her a safe journey. Returning to the greeting party, he apologized, "Sorry to have kept you waiting."

The man was Dr. Albert Schweitzer, the famous missionary doctor who had spent his life helping the poor in Africa. In response to Schweitzer's action, one member of the reception committee said with great admiration to the reporter standing next to him, "That's the first time I ever saw a sermon walking."

Therefore all things whatsoever ye would that men should do to you, do ye even so to them: for this is the law and the prophets.

MATTHEW 7:12

Hard work means nothing to a hen. Regardless of what business prognosticators say about the price of eggs . . . regardless of what others expect of her . . . regardless of fluctuations in the commodities market . . . she keeps on digging worms and laying eggs.

If the ground is hard, she scratches harder.

If it's dry, she digs deeper.

If it's wet, she digs where it is dry.

If she strikes a rock, she digs around it.

If she gets a few more hours of daylight in the barnyard, she digs a few more hours.

Have you ever seen a pessimistic hen?

Have you ever seen a hen cackle in disgust at the prospect of her job?

> *The secret of success is to start from scratch and keep on scratching.*

Did you ever hear one cluck becauses the work was hard, the conditions were poor, and some of her eggs were taken from her before they hatched?

No.

Hens save their breath for digging. They save their cackles for the eggs that are laid.

And the seed in the good soil, these are the ones who have heard the word in an honest and good heart, and hold it fast, and bear fruit with perseverance.
LUKE 8:15 (NASB)

GLDB

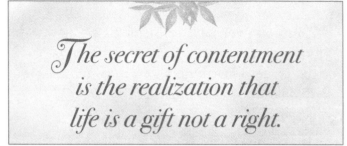

*The secret of contentment
is the realization that
life is a gift not a right.*

At age 14, Andrea Jaeger won her first professional tennis tournament. At 18, she reached the finals at Wimbledon. At 19, a bad shoulder all but ended her career. Many a world-class athlete may have become bitter or discontented with life at that point. Jaeger, however, turned her competitive spirit to a new endeavor, a nonprofit organization called Kids' Stuff Foundation that attempts to bring joy to children suffering from cancer and other life-threatening illnesses. Her work there has also inspired her to take correspondence studies in nursing and child psychology.

Jaeger not only created the program, but runs it full-time, year-round, unpaid. "I'm inspired by these brave kids, and humbled," she has said. "They lose their health, their friends, and sometimes their lives. And yet their spirit never wavers. They look at life as a gift. The rest of us sometimes look at ourselves as a gift to life."

"You get very spoiled on the tour," she adds with a twinkle in her eye. "The courtesy cars, the five-star hotels, the thousands of people clapping for you when you hit a good shot. It's easy to forget what's important in life . . . . I forget a lot less lately."

But godliness with contentment is great gain.
For we brought nothing into this world, and
it is certain we can carry nothing out.
1 TIMOTHY 6:6,7

Dutch author and priest Henri Nouwen admits in his book *In the Name of Jesus* that he felt as if he was in a "rut" in his life for more than twenty years. Nouwen seemed to have it made, with an outstanding academic résumé and noble field of study. Yet, he said, "As I entered into my fifties . . . I came face-to-face with a simple question, "Did becoming older bring me closer to Jesus? After twenty-five years of priesthood, I found myself praying poorly, living somewhat isolated from other people, and very much preoccupied with burning issues . . . . I woke up one day with the realization that I was living in a very dark place."

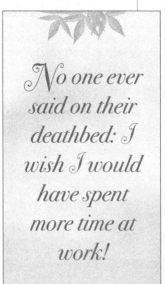

No one ever said on their deathbed: I wish I would have spent more time at work!

Nouwen asked God to show him where He wanted him to go and the Lord made it clear to him that he should leave his prestigious role as a distinguised professor and join the L'Arche communities for mentally handicapped people. In Nouwen's words, "God said, 'Go and live among the poor in spirit, and they will heal you.'" So he did. He faced numerous lessons, some painful, a few humiliating, but in all, he learned how to be a humble servant and a compassionate, caring friend. Nouwen came to realize: it's not work that makes a person, but rather, relationships.

Yea, I hated all my labor which I had taken under the sun: because I should leave it unto the man that shall be after me.
ECCLESIASTES 2:18

And whatsoever ye do, do it heartily, as to the Lord, and not unto men.
COLOSSIANS 3:23

True faith and courage are like a kite—an opposing wind raises it higher.

Norma Zimmer, the well-known singer for Lawrence Welk, had a difficult childhood as a result of her parents' drinking. Singing was her escape! As a high school senior, Norma was invited to be a featured soloist at the University Christian Church in Seattle. When her parents heard she was going to sing a particular song, they both insisted on attending the service. She tells about that morning, "I stole glances at the congregation, trying to find my parents . . . then in horror I saw them—weaving down the aisle in a state of disheveled intoxication. They were late. Few empty seats were left . . . . The congregation stared. I didn't know how I ever got through that morning."

After she sang and took her seat, her heart pounding and her cheeks burning from embarrassment, the pastor preached: "God is our refuge and strength, a tested help in time of trouble." She says, "My own trouble seemed to bear down on me with tremendous weight . . . I realized how desperate life in our family was without God, and that day I recommitted my life to Him . . . Jesus came into my life not only as Savior but for daily strength and direction."

Don't let a difficult time box you in. Let it drive you to Jesus.

But they that wait upon the LORD shall renew their strength; they shall mount up with wings as eagles; they shall run, and not be weary; and they shall walk, and not faint.
ISAIAH 40:31

As a professional stock-car racer, Darrell Waltrip was once proud of his image as "the guy folks loved to hate." When crowds booed, he'd just kick the dirt and smile. Then things began to change. He miraculously survived a Daytona 500 crash. He began going to church with his wife, Stevie. He and Stevie began to try to have a family. Stevie, however, suffered four miscarriages.

In order to receive the direction from God you must be able to receive the correction from God.

One day their pastor came to visit. He asked, "Your car is sponsored by a beer company. Is that the image you want?" Darrell had never thought about it. He had always loved watching kids admire his car, but the more he thought about it, he discovered that he *did* care about his image. He thought, *If Stevie's and my prayers were answered for a child, what kind of dad would I be?* He remembered his pastor's admonition to "walk the walk, not just talk the talk."

He didn't know what to do to convince the car owner to change sponsors, but amazingly, an opportunity opened for him to sign with a new racing team sponsored by a laundry detergent company. After much thought and prayer, he switched teams. Two years later, daughter Jessica was born, and a few years later, daughter Sarah. In 1989, he won at Daytona.

My son, despise not thou the chastening of the Lord, nor faint when thou art rebuked of him: For whom the Lord loveth he chasteneth, and scourgeth every son whom he receiveth.
HEBREWS 12:5,6

> *Those who bring sunshine to the lives of others cannot keep it from themselves.*

The story is told of a man and woman who gave a sizeable contribution to their church to honor the memory of their son who lost his life in the war. When the announcement was made to the congregation of the generous donation, a woman whispered to her husband, "Let's give the same amount in honor of each of our boys."

The husband replied, "What are you talking about? Neither one of our sons was killed in the war."

"Exactly," said the woman. "Let's give it as an expression of our gratitude to God for sparing their lives!"

What we give to charitable concerns during our life produces benefit in three directions:

(1) it helps those in need, (2) it inspires others to give, and, (3) it forms an inner character in the giver—one marked by less selfishness and fewer materialistic tendencies, greater generosity and a heightened awareness of and concern for other people.

Keep in mind that when you give, you are ultimately giving to *people,* even though your gift might be made to an institution or organization. Churches and other charities are made up of people. Your giving brings sunshine to the lives of others and will return to you.

Be not deceived; God is not mocked:
for whatsoever a man soweth,
that shall he also reap.

GALATIANS 6:7

A dog once wandered to a preacher's home, and his three sons played with it, fed it, and soon became quite fond of it. It so happened that the dog had three white hairs on its tail. One day, the preacher and his sons spotted an advertisement in the city newspaper about a lost dog. The description of the stray they had taken in matched perfectly.

The minister later said, "In the presence of my three boys, we carefully separated the three white hairs and removed them from the dog's tail."

No man ever really finds out what he believes in until he begins to instruct his children.

The real owner of the dog eventually discovered where his stray pooch had gone and came to claim him. The dog showed every sign of recognizing his owner, so the man was ready to take him away. At that point, the minister spoke up and asked, "Didn't you say the dog would be known by three white hairs in its tail?" The owner, unable to find the identifying feature, was forced to admit that this dog didn't fully fit the description of his lost dog and he left.

Years passed and the minister noted with sadness, "We kept the dog, but I lost my three boys for Christ that day." His sons no longer had confidence in what their father professed to be true.

Remember, your children watch the choices you make in all areas of your life and base their opinion of you on them. Be a person of integrity—one they will admire.

And, ye fathers, provoke not your children to wrath: but bring them up in the nurture and admonition of the Lord.
EPHESIANS 6:4

> *Don't mistake activity for achievement. Busyness does not equal productiveness.*

In April 1973, the Park Center YMCA in Midland, Texas, asked for volunteers to help repair seventeen run-down homes in the city. The effort was so successful that Midlanders made it an annual event. After volunteers had completed repairs on one home, the owner opened her front door and exclaimed, "It's just like Christmas in April." The name stuck.

"Christmas in April," has not only made hundreds of homes more livable in this West Texas oil town, but it helped bring the city together. Men and women, young and old, black, Hispanic, and white volunteers build community spirit as they scrape, caulk, plaster, paint, hammer, and roof together. Said one volunteer, "It's a blessing to us as well as to those we help. There's no better way to get to know someone than to sit up on a roof with him all day." One year 398 gallons of paint, 600 pounds of nails, 224 squares of roofing materials, 60 doors, and $10,000 of lumber were used to repair 84 homes.

Midlanders have learned how to be *both* busy and productive by pulling together to help others. In most instances of our lives, work need not be left undone or goals sacrificed. Priorities simply need to be realigned.

But Martha was cumbered about much serving, and came to him, and said, Lord, dost thou not care that my sister hath left me to serve alone? bid her therefore that she help me. And Jesus answered and said unto her, "Martha, Martha, thou art careful and troubled about many things: But one thing is needful: and Mary hath chosen that good part, which shall not be taken away from her."

LUKE 10:40-42

Several centuries ago, the Emperor of Japan commissioned a Japanese artist to paint a particular species of bird for him. Months passed, then years. Finally, the Emperor went personally to the artist's studio to ask for an explanation.

The artist set a blank canvas on the easel and within fifteen minutes, had completed a painting of a bird. It was a masterpiece! The Emperor, admiring both the painting and the artist's great skill, asked why there had been such a long delay.

The artist then went from cabinet to cabinet in his studio. He pulled

It's the little things in life that determine the big things.

from its armloads of drawings of feathers, tendons, wings, feet, claws, eyes, beaks— virtually every aspect of the bird, from virtually every angle. He placed these silently before the Emperor, who nodded in understanding.

The magnificence of any "whole" can never be greater than the magnificence of any singular detail.

To have an excellent life, strive for an excellent year. Within that year, strive for an excellent month, and within that month, strive for an excellent day. Within the day, strive for an excellent hour. An excellent life is the sum of many excellent moments!

. . . Thou hast been faithful over a few things, I will make thee ruler over many things: enter thou into the joy of the Lord.

MATTHEW 25:21

> *The doors of opportunity are marked "Push" and "Pull."*

A man once went with a friend for a ride out in the country. They drove off the main road and through a grove of orange trees to a mostly uninhabited piece of land. A few horses grazed there amidst a couple of old shacks. Walter stopped the car and began to describe vividly the things he was going to build on the land. He wanted his friend Arthur to buy some of the acreage surrounding his project. Walter explained to his friend, "I can handle the main project myself. It will take all my money, but . . . I want you to have the first chance at this surrounding acreage, because in the next five years it will increase in value several hundred times."

Arthur thought to himself, *Who in the world is going to drive twenty-five miles for this crazy project? His dream has taken the best of his common sense.* He mumbled something about a tight-money situation and promised to look into the deal later. "Later on will be too late," Walter cautioned. "You'd better move on it right now." Arthur failed, however, to act.

And so it was that Art Linkletter turned down the opportunity to buy the land that surrounded what became Disneyland, the land his friend Walt Disney had tried to talk him into.

Most opportunities take a step of faith whether for financial or relational investments.

The soul of the sluggard desireth,
and hath nothing: but the soul
of the diligent shall be made fat.

PROVERBS 13:4

Novelist A. J. Cronin had been in practice as a physician for almost ten years when he developed a gastric ulcer that required complete rest. He went to a farm in the Scottish Highlands to recuperate. He says, "The first few days of leisure were pleasant enough, but soon the enforced idleness of Fyne Farm became insufferable . . . . I had often, in the back of my mind, nursed the vague illusion that I might write. I had actually thought out the theme of a novel—the tragic record of a man's egotism and bitter pride . . . .

You cannot win if you do not begin.

"Upstairs in my cold, clean bedroom was a scrubbed deal table and a very hard chair. Next morning I found myself in this chair, facing a new exercise book open upon the table, slowly becoming aware that, short of Latin prescriptions, I had never composed a significant phrase in all my life. It was a discouraging thought as I picked up my pen. "Never mind, I began."

Even though Cronin struggled to write 500 words a day and eventually threw his first draft on the farm's trash heap, he finished *Hatter's Castle*. The book was dramatized, translated into 22 languages, and sold some five million copies. The world had lost a physician, but gained a novelist.

Now therefore perform the doing of it;
that as there was a readiness to will,
so there may be a performance
also out of that which ye have.
2 CORINTHIANS 8:11

> *The best way to be successful
> is to follow the advice
> you give others.*

An officer in the navy had dreamed from childhood of commanding a great battleship one day. He finally achieved his dream and was given commission of the newest and proudest ship in the fleet.

One stormy night, the captain was on duty on the bridge when he spotted a strange light rapidly closing in on his own vessel. As his ship plowed through the giant waves, the light rose and fell just above the horizon of the sea. He ordered his signalman to flash a message to the unidentified craft on his port side, "Alter your course ten degrees to the south."

Within seconds a reply came, "Alter your course ten degrees to the north." Determined that his ship would never take a backseat to any other, the captain snapped a second order, "Alter course ten degrees—I am the CAPTAIN!" The response was beamed back, "Alter your course ten degrees—I am Seaman Third Class Smith." By this time, the light was growing ever brighter and larger.

Infuriated, the captain grabbed the signal light and personally signaled, "Alter course. I am a battleship." The reply came just as quickly, "Alter your course. I am a lighthouse."

He who ignores discipline despises himself, but whoever heeds correction gains understanding.
PROVERBS 15:32 (NIV)

The story is told of a farmer who had lived on the same farm all his life. It was a good farm with fertile soil, but with the passing of years, the farmer began to think, *Maybe there's something better for me.* He set out to find an even better plot of land to farm.

Every day he found a new reason for criticizing some feature of his old farm. Finally, he decided to sell. He listed the farm with a real estate broker who promptly prepared an advertisement emphasizing all the many advantages of the acreage: ideal location, modern equipment, healthy stock, acres of fertile ground, high yield crops, well-kept barns and pens, nice two-story house on a hill above the pasture.

Contentment isn't getting what we want but being satisfied with what we have.

When the real estate agent called to read the ad to the farmer for his approval prior to placing it in the local paper, the farmer heard him out. When he had finished, he cried, "Hold everything! I've changed my mind. I'm not going to sell. Why, I've been looking for a place just like that all my life!"

When you start identifying the good traits of any person, situation or organization, you are likely to find that they far outweigh the bad. Focus on what you have. What you have *not* will likely seem less insignificant.

Not that I speak in respect of want;
for I have learned, in whatsoever
state I am, therewith to be content.
PHILIPPIANS 4:11

> *Too many people
> quit looking for work
> when they find a job.*

In her autobiography, *Who Could Ask For Anything More,* Ethel Merman tells how Cole Porter and a buddy of his had a game they played with Irving Berlin. Says Merman, "When they see Irving coming they look at their wrist watches and make a five-dollar bet. Then they pick a topic and start in on it. Anything will do: Victor Moore, Mount Everest, volcanoes, Eskimo Pies, Philadelphia, the Dalai Lama of Tibet. The bet is based on the number of minutes it will take Irving to bring the conversation around to one of his own songs, no matter where it starts. The average time is said to be less than five minutes."

Merman notes, "I wouldn't go so far as to call this ego on Irving's part. It's just that he's so absorbed in his work and so intense about it that what he writes is the most important thing in the world to him . . . . To me, he doesn't seem so much egotistical as enthusiastic."

Interesting that Cole Porter would play such a trick since he once told an interviewer, "If I don't seem to be listening to what you're saying, it's because I'm writing a song in the back of my head . . . . Some people think work is a four-letter word. I don't."

He also that is slothful in his work is brother to him that is a great waster.

PROVERBS 18:9

In the mid nineteenth century, tea cost about a dollar a pound, making it an expensive staple. George Hartford and George Gilman came up with a simple but revolutionary plan to lower the price. They bought tea directly from the ships in New York Harbor. Then, taking a low-percentage profit, they tried to achieve high-volume sales. Their tactics worked. They soon turned their mail-order business into a chain of stores called the Great Atlantic and Pacific Tea Co.—A&P.

You can't take your money with you, but you can send it on ahead.

From the outset, and even with a family of five children, Hartford generously gave thousands of dollars a year to charitable causes, ranging from the Pius X Mission in Skagway, Alaska, to the First Methodist church in Urbana, Illinois. As his fortune increased, he established a foundation as a conduit for his giving. Hartford's desire was that his contributions benefit people such as those whose purchases at A&P stores had built his fortune. Later, he reorganized the foundation to receive his estate, so that by the time he died, bequests to individuals totaled $500,000, with $55 million going to the foundation, including $40 million in A&P stock. Thus, a portion of every dollar spent at an A&P store would eventually be "donated." Hartford in many ways is *still* giving his fortune away!

Lay not up for yourselves treasures upon earth, where moth and rust doth corrupt, and where thieves break through and steal: But lay up for yourselves treasures in heaven, where neither moth nor rust doth corrupt, and where thieves do not break through nor steal.

MATTHEW 6:19,20

> *Ability will enable a man to go to the top, but it takes character to keep him there.*

Convicted Watergate conspirator John Ehrlichman wrote of his experience: "When I went to jail, nearly two years after the cover-up trial; I had a big self-esteem problem. I was a felon, shorn and scorned, clumping around in a ragged old army uniform, doing pick and shovel work out on the desert. I wondered if anyone thought I was worth anything . . . . For years I had been able to sweep most of my shortcomings and failures under the rug and not face them, but during the two long criminal trials, I spent my days listening to prosecutors tell juries what a bad fellow I was . . . I'd go back to a hotel room and sit alone thinking about what was happening to me. During that time I began to take stock . . . . I was wiped out. I had nothing left that had been of value to me—honor, credibility, virtue, recognition, profession."

Then he began to see himself . . . and to care deeply about his own integrity, his capacity to love and be loved, and his essential worth. He concluded about the Nixon years, "In a paradoxical way, I'm grateful for them. Somehow I had to see all of that and grow to understand it in order to arrive." Sadly, the inner character Ehrlichman developed came too late to impact his political career at the top.

Keep a daily check on your character. Of all the abilities you may possess, the one to develop a good character is your greatest.

The righteousness of the blameless makes a straight way for them, but the wicked are brought down by their own wickedness.
PROVERBS 11:5 (NIV)

Author J. Allan Petersen tells about a flight he took on a 747 out of Brazil. He was awakened from sleep by a strong voice announcing, "We have a very serious emergency." Three engines had quit because of fuel contamination and the fourth was expected to go at any second. The plane began to drop and turn in the night, preparing for an emergency landing.

At first the situation seemed unreal to Petersen, but when the steward barked, "Prepare for impact," he found himself—and everyone around him praying. As he buried his head in his lap and pulled up his knees, he said, "Oh, God, thank You. Thank You for the incredible privilege of knowing You. Life has been wonderful." As the plane approached the

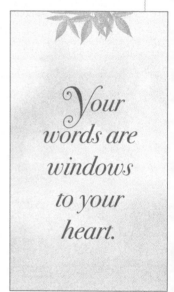

Your words are windows to your heart.

ground, his last cry was, "Oh, God, my wife! My children!"

Petersen survived. As he wandered about the airport in a daze, aching all over, he found he couldn't speak, but his mind was racing, *What were my last words? What was the bottom line?* As he remembered, he had his answer: relationship. Reunited with his wife and sons, he found that all he could say to them over and over was, "I appreciate you, I appreciate you!"

Listen to what you are saying. Have you told that person who matters most to you how you *really* feel?

. . . For out of the abundance of the heart the mouth speaketh.
MATTHEW 12:34

> # A shut mouth gathers no foot.

Constance Cameron tells a lesson her mother taught her. One day, when she was about eight, she was playing beside an open window. Inside, Mrs. Brown was confiding a personal problem to Constance's mother. After Mrs. Brown had gone, the mother realized that Constance had heard everything that had been said. She called her in and said, "If Mrs. Brown had left her purse here today, would we give it to anyone else?"

"Of course not," the girl said. Her mother went on, "Mrs. Brown left something more precious than her pocketbook today. She left a story that could make many people unhappy. The story is not ours to give to anyone. It is still hers, even though she left it here. So we shall not give it to anyone. Do you understand?"

She did. And from that day on, whenever a friend would share a confidence or even engage in careless gossip, she considered what they said to be the personal property of the other person—and not hers to give to anyone else.

The old saying bears great truth: "If you don't have something positive to say about someone or something, don't say anything."

He that keepeth his mouth keepeth his life: but he that openeth wide his lips shall have destruction.
PROVERBS 13:3

When Charles Spurgeon was still a boy preacher, he was warned about a certain woman with a reputation for being extremely quarrelsome. He was told that she intended to give him a tongue-lashing the moment she saw him next.

Spurgeon said, "All right, but that's a game two can play."

Shortly thereafter she met him and began to assault him with a flood of verbal abuse. He simply smiled back at her and said, "Oh, yes, thank you. I am quite well. Thank you for asking. I hope you are the same."

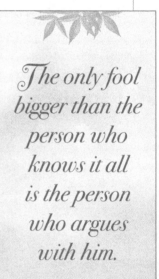

The only fool bigger than the person who knows it all is the person who argues with him.

His remarks were followed by another tirade of know-it-all comments, this time voiced at a slightly higher volume. He responded again, smiling quietly, "Yes, it does look rather as if it might rain. I think I had better be getting on."

"Bless the man!" the woman exclaimed and then concluded, "He's as deaf as a post. What's the use of storming at him!"

Never again did she assault Spurgeon with her arguments. And never did he tell her what he had done! There's no point in arguing with know-it-all people. Better to let them have their say and walk on.

*He that reproveth a scorner getteth
to himself shame: and he that rebuketh
a wicked man getteth himself a blot.*
PROVERBS 9:7

> *A drowning man does not complain about the size of a life preserver.*

On his way home to surprise his mother for All Souls' Day, Mishi Dobos stopped by the family's summer cottage to see what repairs he might undertake next. His eyes fell on the garden well, a solid brick structure four feet in diameter. As he leaned over to peer into the 74-foot shaft with a flashlight, he failed to notice the frosty moss on the well's rim. Within seconds, he had plummeted feet first into the shaft, landing ankle-deep in soft mud.

For three days Mishi shouted for help. Then, on the fourth day, while attempting to make a place to sit, he ripped a carpenter's clamp—a foot-long piece of metal with upturned ends—away from the rotting wood. Mishi thought, *What can I do with this?*

Studying the walls, he saw a brick missing on one side. An idea dawned—use the clamp to chip out bricks in a staggered, upward fashion and climb out!

Mishi went to work. At best, he could remove three bricks an hour. But brick by brick and a bad fall later—in all, six days and 23 hours after plunging into the well—Mishi swung his leg over the edge of the upper rim, the rusty carpenter's clamp in his hand.

Look around. What normally useless object might God lead you to use with cleverness and strength?

*Do all things without murmurings
and disputings.*
PHILIPPIANS 2:14

In the 18th century, Dr. Johann Beringer was a professor of natural philosophy at the University of Wurzburg, Germany. He concluded that fossils were not linked previously to living animals, as some were advocating, but rather, they were unique "creations," each part of a divine message planted into the earth by the Lord at the time of Creation. He advocated that man study the fossils with the intent of uncovering the meaning of God's buried message.

> *Blessed is he who, having nothing to say, refrains from giving wordy evidence of the fact.*

His students decided to make and then implant into a nearby hillside, hundreds of grotesque clay forms, some of which were fossil-like, others of which had writing on them. One of the clay figures was actually signed by "Jehovah."

The doctor was so convinced that his "find" had divine meaning that he published a book on the subject, ignoring the repeated confessions of his students as to their prank. He chided his students for attempting to undermine his work and rob him of the fame due to him. It was not until Beringer discovered a "fossil" bearing his own name that he accepted the hoax for what it had been. And for the rest of his life, he spent a small fortune trying to buy back the existing copies of his own book.

The tongue of the wise useth knowledge aright: but the mouth of fools poureth out foolishness.
PROVERBS 15:2

> *Luck: a loser's excuse for a winner's position.*

During the reign of Abdullah the Third, a great drought struck Baghdad. The Mohammedan doctors issued a decree that all the faithful should offer prayers for rain. Still, the drought continued.

The Jews were then permitted to add their prayers. Their supplications also appeared ineffectual. Finally when the drought resulted in widespread famine, the Christians in the land were asked to pray. It also happened that torrents of rain followed almost immediately.

The whole *Conclave* was more upset over the cessation of the drought than it had been alarmed at its continuance. Feeling that some explanation was necessary, they issued this statement to the masses: "The God of our

Prophet was highly gratified by the prayers of the faithful which were as sweet-smelling savors to Him. He refused their requests in order to prolong the pleasure of listening to their prayers; but the prayers of those Christian infidels were an abomination to Him, and He granted their petitions the sooner to be rid of their loathsome importunities."

Be careful how you ridicule a victor. He may have the skill to best you again in yet another contest.

The soul of the sluggard desireth, and hath nothing: but the soul of the diligent shall be made fat.
PROVERBS 13:4

On a summer morning as he was fixing his breakfast, Ray Blankenship looked out his window to see a young girl being swept along in the rain-flooded drainage ditch beside his Ohio home. Blankenship knew that farther downstream, the ditch disappeared with a roar underneath the road and then emptied into the main culvert.

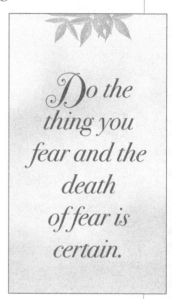

Do the thing you fear and the death of fear is certain.

Ray dashed from his home and raced along the ditch, trying to get ahead of the flailing child. Finally, he hurled himself into the deep, churning water. When he surfaced, he was able to grab the girl's arm. The two tumbled end over end and then, within about three feet of the yawning culvert, Ray's free hand felt something protrude from the bank. He clung to it desperately, the tremendous force of the water trying to tear him and the child away.

By the time the fire-department rescuers arrived, Blankenship amazingly had pulled the girl to safety. Both were treated for shock. In that heroic moment, Ray Blankenship was at even greater risk than most people knew . . . since . . . Ray couldn't swim.

Today, let your courage respond to the needs that you see, not the fear that you may feel.

Be strong and of good courage, fear not, nor be afraid of them: for the LORD thy God, he it is that doth go with thee; he will not fail thee, nor forsake thee.
DEUTERONOMY 31:6

GLDB

> # *G*od plus one is always
> a majority!

Wishing to encourage her young son's progress at the piano, a mother bought tickets to an Ignace Paderewski performance. When the night arrived, the two found their seats near the front of the concert hall. The boy stared wide-eyed in amazement at the majestic grand piano on the stage. The mother began talking to a friend sitting nearby and she failed to notice her son slip away. As the house lights dimmed and the spotlight lit the piano, the woman gasped as she saw her son at the piano bench, innocently picking out "Twinkle, Twinkle, Little Star."

Before the woman could retrieve her son, the famous concert pianist appeared on stage and quickly moved to the keyboard. "Don't quit—keep playing," he whispered to the boy. Leaning over, Paderewski reached down with his left hand and began filling in a bass part. Then with his right arm, he reached around the other side, encircling the child, to add a running obligato. Together the old master and the young novice mesmerized the crowd.

No matter how insignificant or "amateur-ish" you may feel today, the Master has these words for you, "Don't quit—keep playing." He will add whatever is needed to turn your efforts into a masterpiece.

If God be for us, who can be against us?
ROMANS 8:31

In 1752, a group of Methodist men, including John Wesley, signed a covenant which every man agreed to hang on his study wall. The six articles of this solemn agreement were as follows:

1. That we will not listen or willingly inquire after ill concerning one another;

2. That, if we do hear any ill of each other, we will not be forward to believe it;

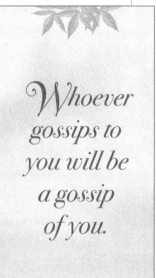

Whoever gossips to you will be a gossip of you.

3. That as soon as possible we will communicate what we heard by speaking or writing to the person concerned;

4. That until we have done this, we will not write or speak a syllable of it to any other person;

5. That neither will we mention it, after we have done this, to any other person;

6. That we will not make any exception to any of these rules unless we think ourselves absolutely obliged in conference.

Talk about an Anti-Gossip Pact!

Always remember: the person who tells you "don't tell this to a soul" has probably told all the souls you know.

A talebearer revealeth secrets: but he that is of a faithful spirit concealeth a matter.

PROVERBS 11:13

> *Jesus is a friend who knows all your faults and still loves you anyway.*

Matthew was a tax collector, a hated man among the Jews for helping Rome tighten its occupation. Even so . . . Jesus loved Matthew, and eventually chose him as one of his apostles.

Peter had a quick temper, his emotions easily triggered by circumstances. He denied knowing Jesus three times during the most critical hours of Jesus' life on earth. Even so . . . Jesus loved Peter and empowered him to lead the early church.

Saul "made havoc" of the church in Jerusalem, leading raids on the homes of Christians and imprisoning the devout. He consented to the death of Stephen, and was one of the official witnesses of his execution. He even requested letters of authority to extend the persecution of the church to other cities, including Damascus. Even so . . . Jesus loved Saul, appeared to him in a light from heaven, and called him to repentance.

No matter what a person may have done—no matter their character flaws—Jesus loves them. He loved them to the point of dying on their behalf on the Cross . . . including dying for your enemy . . . the friend or family member who disappoints you or frustrates you . . . indeed, including you.

But God commendeth his love toward us, in that, while we were yet sinners, Christ died for us.
ROMANS 5:8

An old legend tells of a covey of quail that lived in a forest. They would have been happy except for their enemy, the quail catcher. He would imitate their call, and then when they gathered together, he would throw a net over them, stuff them into his hunting basket, and carry them off to market.

One wise quail said, "Brothers, I have a plan. When the fowler puts his net over us, we each should put our head into a section of the net and begin to flap our wings. We can lift the net together and fly away with it." All agreed. The next day, they did just that, making a successful escape. After several days, the fowler's wife asked him, "Where are the quail to take to market?" he replied, "The trouble is that all the birds work together and help one another escape."

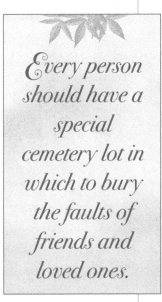

Every person should have a special cemetery lot in which to bury the faults of friends and loved ones.

Awhile later, one quail began to fight with another. "I lifted all the weight on the net. You didn't help at all," he cried. The other quail became angry and before long, the entire covey was quarreling. The fowler saw his chance. He imitated the cry of the quail and cast his net over them. Preoccupied with their quarreling, they didn't help one another and lift the net in flight. Sometimes pointing out the faults of others can "do us in" as well.

And be ye kind one to another, tenderhearted, forgiving one another, even as God for Christ's sake hath forgiven you.
EPHESIANS 4:32

Ignorance is always swift to speak.

One of the favorite stories of Arturo Toscanini, the great symphony conductor, was this:

An orchestra was playing Beethoven's Leonore overture, which has two great musical climaxes. Each of these musical high points is followed by a trumpet passage, which the composer intended to be played offstage.

The first climax arrived, but no sound came from a trumpet offstage. The conductor, annoyed, went on to the second musical high point. But again—no trumpet could be heard.

This time, the conductor rushed into the wings, fuming and with every intent of demanding a full explanation. There he found the trumpet player struggling with the house security man who was insisting as he held for dear life onto the man's trumpet, "I tell you, you can't play that trumpet back here! You'll disturb the rehearsal!"

Until you know *why* someone is acting the way they do, it's better not to criticize him. Until you know who has told him to act, it's better not to attempt to stop him!

Let every man be swift to hear,
slow to speak, slow to wrath.
JAMES 1:19

In his autobiography, Lee Iacocca gives others an opportunity to learn from a mistake he once made. In 1956, Ford emphasized auto safety rather than performance and horse-power. The company introduced crash padding for dashboards and sent out a film to explain how much safer the new dashboards were. The narrator on the film claimed the padding was so thick a person could drop an egg on it from a two-story building and it would bounce right off without breaking. As a district assistant sales manager for Ford, Iacocca decided he'd demonstrate this fact!

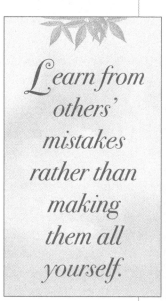

Learn from others' mistakes rather than making them all yourself.

With 1,100 salemen watching him, he climbed a high ladder and proceeded to drop an egg on a strip of the dash padding he had placed on the floor of the stage. The egg missed the padding and splattered on the floor. A second egg bounced off his assistant's shoulder. Eggs three and four landed on target, but broke on impact. Finally, with the fifth egg, he got the desired result. Iacocca writes, "I learned two lessons that day. First, never use eggs in a sales rally. And second, never go before customers without rehearsing what you want to say—as well as what you're going to *do*—to help sell your product."

Good advice!

The way of a fool is right in his own eyes:
but he that hearkeneth unto counsel is wise.
PROVERBS 12:15

> ## *Pick your friends but not to pieces.*

A trumpeter was once captured by the enemy. He pleaded with his captors: "Please spare me! I have no gun. I am not guilty of any crime. I have not killed a single one of your soldiers. I only carry this poor brass trumpet and play it when I'm told to."

"That is the very reason for putting you to death," his captors said. "For, while you do not fight yourself, your trumpet stirs up all the others to battle. It causes many others to kill!"

So it is with our criticism of others. We may not hate, mistrust, or avoid the person we criticize, but our criticism can cause others to manifest these feelings and behaviors.

There once was a woman to whom gossip and criticism were so utterly distasteful that whenever a visitor brought up something negative about a person, she would say, "Come, let's go and ask if this is true." The tale-bearer was always so taken aback that he or she would beg to be excused. But the determined woman would insist on escorting the reluctant soul to the subject of the tale to verify its truth or to hear the other point of view. After awhile, no one repeated a tale or voiced a criticism in her presence!

Build up your friends . . . don't tear them down!

A man that beareth false witness
against his neighbor is a maul,
and a sword, and a sharp arrow.
PROVERBS 25:18

R. G. LeTourneau, an outstanding Christian businessman for whom LeTourneau College was named, made a fortune with a company that manufactured large earthmoving equipment. He once remarked, "We used to make a scraper known as 'Model G.' One day somebody asked our salesman what the G stood for. The man, who was pretty quick on the trigger, immediately replied, 'I'll tell you. The G stands for gossip because like a talebearer this machine moves a lot of dirt and moves it fast.'"

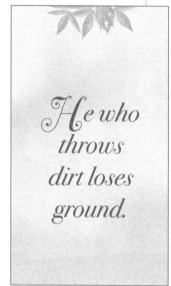

He who throws dirt loses ground.

The trouble with gossip is not so much that it is spoken as an intended lie, but that it is *heard* as if it were the absolute truth. Abraham Lincoln had a favorite riddle he used to put to people. "If a man were to call the tail of a dog a leg, how many legs would the dog have?"

The usual reply was "five."

"Wrong," Lincoln would say with his wry smile. "The dog still has four legs. Calling the tail a leg doesn't make it one."

Just because a tale may have been repeated many times by so-called "reliable sources" doesn't necessarily make it true.

Wherefore putting away lying, speak every man truth with his neighbor: for we are members one of another.
EPHESIANS 4:25

> *You don't have to lie awake nights to succeed – just stay awake days.*

Entrepreneur Victor Kiam, perhaps most famour for promoting electric razors in recent years, once worked as a salesman for Lever Brothers. If he was going to be selling in a particular town, Kiam liked to arrive there the night before so he could get a good night's sleep and start his appointments early. If he couldn't find a hotel room, he'd sleep in his car.

On one of his trips to Baton Rouge, he arrived at 1 A.M. and found no room at any inn. He parked on the side of a country road and flopped into the backseat. At about 3 A.M. he was awakened by a policemen knocking on the car window. He told the policeman what he was doing and found him very sympathetic. "If anything happened to you I wouldn't forgive myself," the policeman said. "I'll tell you what. Why don't you come down to the jailhouse and sleep in one of the cells? You can get up and go as soon as you wake up."

And so Kiam spent the night in an unlocked cell. The next morning the policeman treated him to coffee, ham and eggs, and a sweet roll. He says, "They ran a very nice establishment. I liked the place so much I wished I could have bought it."

Kiam not only was willing to work long days, but also was clever in making his "nights" work for him!

I must work the works of him that sent me, while it is day: the night cometh, when no man can work.

JOHN 9:4

Helen Keller was left deaf and blind by an incurable childhood illness. A patient and persistent teacher, Anne Sullivan, taught her to read through her senses of touch, smell and taste.

At the close of her autobiography Helen Keller writes:

Fate—silent, pitiless—bars the way. Fain would I question his imperious decree; for my heart is undisciplined and passionate, but my tongue will not utter the bitter, futile words that rise to my lips, and they back into my heart like unshed tears. Silence sits immense upon my soul. Then comes hope with a smile and whispers, "There is joy in self-forgetfulness." So I try to make the light in other people's eyes my sun, the music in

The first step to wisdom is silence; the second is listening.

other's ears my symphony, the smile on other's lips my happiness.

Silence can be used to nurture pouting, anger, and hatred. Far better uses for silence are reflecting, meditating, and listening. It is only when we are truly silent before the Lord that we can hear His still small voice speaking in our souls.

A wise man will hear, and will increase learning; and a man of understanding shall attain unto wise counsels.

PROVERBS 1:5

> *The greatest possession you have is the 24 hours directly in front of you.*

Dr. C.C. Albertson once wrote this about the use of time: "It might be wise for us to take a little inventory of our resources as to time and review our habits of using it. There are 168 hours in each week. Fifty-six of them we spend in sleep. Of the remaining 112 hours, we devote 48 to labor. This leaves 64 hours, of which let us assign 12 hours for our daily meals . . . .

"We have left 52 hours, net, of conscious active life to devote to any purpose to which we are inclined.

"Is it too much to say that God requires a tithe of his peoples' free time? One tenth of 52 hours is 5.2 hours. How much of this tithe of time do we devote to strictly religious uses?"

If one allowed an hour for church and an hour for a Bible study or prayer meeting each week, he would still have 192 minutes a week—enough for nearly a half hour each day in prayer and Bible reading. Such a person would still have more than 45 hours a week for life's chores and personal fun!

The old excuse, "I have too little time," doesn't fly. What is more likely the case is this: too little planning of the time we have!

There is a time there for every
purpose and for every work.
ECCLESIASTES 3:17

In his autobiography, Armand Hammer—known as much for his humanitarian efforts as for being chairman and CEO of Occidental Petroleum, an advisor to presidents from Roosevelt to Reagan, and an industrialist—reveals the roots of his giving spirit:

"My father had become a prominent and greatly loved figure in the area . . . . It was an almost ecstatic experience for me to ride with him when he went on his doctor's rounds . . . patients at their doors greeted him with such warmth that waves of

The most valuable gift you can give another is a good example.

pride and honor would surge in me to find myself the son of such a father, a man so obviously good, so obviously deserving of the affection he received.

"He could have made himself many times richer, however, if he had insisted on collecting all his bills; or if he could have restrained himself from giving money away; but then he would not have been the man he was . . . I have seen, in his office, drawers full of unpaid bills for which he refused to demand payment because he knew the difficult circumstances of the patients. And I heard innumerable stories from patients about his leaving money behind to pay for the prescriptions he had written when he visited people who were too poor to eat, let alone pay the doctor."

What a wonderful legacy to leave to your child—the "business" of loving and giving to others.

For I have given you an example,
that ye should do as I have done to you.
JOHN 13:15

> *Don't be afraid of pressure.*
> *Remember that pressure*
> *is what turns a lump of*
> *coal into a diamond.*

An old legend says that God first created birds without wings. Sometime later, God made wings and said to the birds, "Come, take up these burdens and bear them." The birds hesitated at first, but soon obeyed. They tried picking up the wings in their beaks, but found them too heavy. Then they tried picking them up with their claws, but found them too large. Finally, one of the birds managed to get the wings hoisted onto its shoulders where it was finally possible to carry them.

To the amazement of the birds, before long the wings began to grow and they soon had attached themselves to the bodies of the birds. One of the birds began to flap his wings and others followed his example. Before long, one of the birds took off and began to soar in the air above!

What had once been a heavy burden now became the very thing that enabled the birds to go where they could never go before . . . and at the same time, truly fulfill the destiny of their creation.

The duties and responsibilities you count as burdens today may be part of God's destiny for your life, the means by which your soul is lifted up and prepared for eternity.

Knowing this, that the trying of our faith worketh patience. But let patience have her perfect work, that ye may be perfect and entire, wanting nothing.

James 1:3,4

When William Gladstone was Chancellor of the Exchequer, he once requested that the Treasury send him certain statistics upon which he might base his budget proposals. The statistician made a mistake. But Gladstone was so certain of this man's concern for accuracy that he didn't take time to verify the figures. As a result, he went before the House of Commons and made a speech based upon the incorrect figures given him. His speech was no sooner published than the inaccuracies were exposed and Gladstone became the brunt of public ridicule.

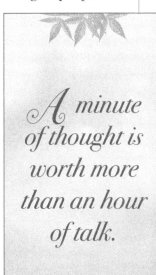

A minute of thought is worth more than an hour of talk.

The Chancellor sent for the statistician who had given him the erroneous information. The man arrived full of fear and shame, certain he was going to be let go. Instead, Gladstone said, "I know how much you must be disturbed over what has happened, and I have sent for you to put you at ease. For a long time you have been engaged in handling the intricacies of the national accounts, and this is the first mistake that you have made. I want to congratulate you, and to express to you my deep appreciation."

It takes a big person to extend mercy . . . a big person to listen rather than talk . . . a big person to think before jumping into action.

Set a watch, O Lord, before my mouth; keep the door of my lips.
PSALM 141:3

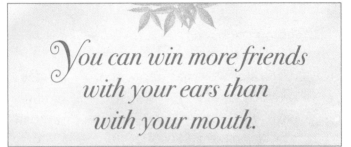

> *You can win more friends
> with your ears than
> with your mouth.*

Rabbi Harold S. Kushner writes in *When All You've Ever Wanted Isn't Enough:*

"A business associate of my father's died under particularly tragic circumstances, and I accompanied my father to the funeral. The man's widow and children were surrounded by clergy and psychiatrists trying to ease their grief and make them feel better. They knew all the right words, but nothing helped. They were beyond being comforted. The widow kept saying, 'You're right, I know you're right, but it doesn't make any difference.' Then a man walked in, a big burly man in his eighties who was a legend in the toy and game industry. He had come to this country illiterate and penniless and had built up an immensely successful company. He was known as a hard bargainer, a ruthless competitor. Despite his success, he had never learned to read or write . . . . He had been sick recently, and his face and his walking showed it. But he walked over to the widow and started to cry, and she cried with him, and you could feel the atmosphere change in the room. This man who had never read a book in his life spoke the language of the heart and held the key that opened the gates of solace where learned doctors and clergy could not."

Let every man be swift to hear;
slow to speak, slow to wrath.
JAMES 1:19

A twelve-year-old boy accepted Jesus Christ as his personal Savior and Lord during a weekend revival meeting. The next week his school friends questioned him about the experience.

"Did you hear God talk?" one asked.

"No," the boy said.

"Did you have a vision?" another asked.

"No," the boy replied.

"Well, how did you know it was God?" a third friend asked.

The boy thought for a moment and then said, "It's like when you catch a fish. You can't see the fish or hear the fish; you just feel him tugging your line. I felt God tugging on my heart."

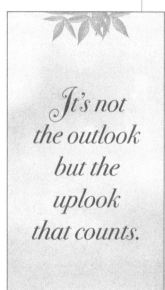

It's not the outlook but the uplook that counts.

So often we try to figure out life by what we can see, hear, or experience with our other senses. We make calculated estimates and judgments based on empirical evidence. There's a level of truth, however, that cannot be perceived by the senses or measured objectively. It's at that level where faith abounds. It is our faith that compels us to *believe,* even when we cannot explain to others why or how or to what specific earthly end. By our faith we only know in Whom we trust. And that is sufficient.

Looking unto Jesus the author
and finisher of our faith.
HEBREWS 12:2

*Put others before yourself,
and you can become
a leader among men.*

The following set of contrasting remarks has been offered as a character sketch of a good leader. For a personal challenge, as you read through the list, circle the descriptive words you believe most closely identify *you!*

Self-reliant but not Self-sufficient
Energetic but not Self-seeking
Steadfast but not Stubborn
Tactful but not timid
Serious but not Sullen
Loyal but not Sectarian
Unmovable but not Stationary
Gentle but not Hypersensitive
Tenderhearted but not Touchy
Conscientious but not a Perfectionist
Disciplined but not Demanding

Generous but not Gullible
Meek but not Weak
Humorous but not Hilarious
Friendly but not Familiar
Holy but not Holier-than-thou
Discerning but not Critical
Progressive but not Pretentious
Authoritative but not Autocratic

Ask God to help you develop in the descriptive words you didn't circle.

But it shall not be so among you:
but whosoever will be great among you,
let him be your minister; and whosoever will
be chief among you, let him be your servant.
MATTHEW 20:26, 27

Richard E. Byrd spent the winter of 1934 at Bolling Advance Weather Base in Antarctica, where the temperature ranged from -58° to -76° F. By the time he was rescued, he was suffering from frostbite and carbon monoxide poisoning. He wrote in his book, *Alone:* "I had hardly strength to move. I clung to the sleeping bag, which was the only source of comfort and warmth left to me and mournfully debated the little that might be done. Two facts stood clear. One was that my chances of recovering were slim. The other was that in my weakness I was incapable of taking care of myself. *But you must have faith—you must have faith in the outcome,* I whispered to myself. It is like a flight . . . into another unknown. You start and you cannot turn back.

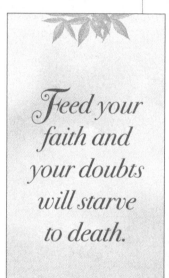

Feed your faith and your doubts will starve to death.

You must go on . . . trusting your instruments, the course you have plotted.

With faith as his only guidance system, Byrd forced himself to do the necessary things for survival *very slowly* and with *great deliberation*. At times he felt as if he were living a thousand years in any given minute. But at each days' end, he could say he was still alive. And that was enough.

Some times the only thing left to do in a situation is to press on in faith. And so . . . press on!

*But we are not of those who shrink back
to destruction, but of those who have
faith to the preserving of the soul.*
HEBREWS 10:39 (NASB)

> ## Never pass up a chance to keep your mouth shut.

President Calvin Coolidge, the thirtieth president of the United States, was a reserved man who spoke very little. A reporter attempted to interview him, and the conversation went as follows:

Reporter: Do you wish to say anything about the war threat in Europe?

Coolidge: No.

Reporter: About the strike in the clothing factories?

Coolidge: No.

Reporter: About the League of Nations?

Coolidge: No.

Reporter: About the farm production problem?

Coolidge: No.

As the reporter began to leave the room, Coolidge unexpectedly called back to him and said, "Don't quote me."

Never let yourself feel pressured into saying something you don't want to say, or into saying something when you don't feel like talking. Silence is not a "lack" of communication. It is a form of communication, and it can be a very effective one at that.

Even a fool, when he holdeth his peace, is counted wise: and he that shutteth his lips is esteemed a man of understanding.

PROVERBS 17:28

The story is told of a boy and his mother who went to a shopping mall. The boy acted badly—demanding this and that, running away from his mother, hiding so she couldn't find him, whining that he wanted something to eat or drink, interrupting her while she was attempting to talk to sales clerks or make a purchase. In total exasperation, she finally gave up and returned to the car.

As they were driving home, the boy could sense her displeasure and he said, "I learned last week in Sunday school that when we ask God to forgive us when we are bad, He does. Does he really do that?"

The mother replied, "Yes, He does." The boy continued, "And the teacher said that when He forgives us, He throws ours sins

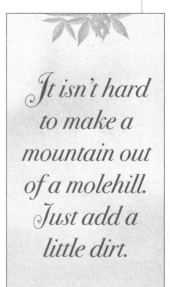

It isn't hard to make a mountain out of a molehill. Just add a little dirt.

into the deepest sea. Does he do that, Mom?" The mother responded, "Yes, that's what the Bible says."

The boy was silent for a moment and then he said, "I've asked God to forgive me for acting bad at the mall, but I bet when we get home, you're going to go fishing for those sins, aren't you?"

Surely one of the best ways to avoid a quarrel with a person is to avoid going fishing for their past sins!

Starting a quarrel is like breaching a dam; so drop the matter before a dispute breaks out.

PROVERBS 17:14 (NIV)

GLDB

> *What counts is not the number of hours that you put in, but how much you put in the hours.*

In 1930, Pat O'Brien had a scene in a play *The Up and Up* in which he had to contend with two angry people at once—a person on the phone and one at his desk. To him, playing the scene was "like fighting through Notre Dame's football line while singing 'Danny Boy.' " The play received mixed reviews and its outlook seemed dim. O'Brien thought, *Why knock myself out on something with no future?* But then a Bible verse echoed in his memory: "Whatever task lies to your hand, do it with all your might" (Eccl. 9:10). And so, at every performance, he put his all into that scene, sometimes coming off stage wringing wet.

After the show closed, O'Brien went on to a few obscure parts. Then one day he received a phone call from a man who said, "Mr. Hughes is filming the play *The Front Page* and wants you in it." O'Brien jumped at the opportunity. The film's director, Lewis Milestone, later told him why he was chosen. Milestone had gone to New York with friends, planning to see a hit show, but they were one seat short so Lewis went to see *The Up and Up*. He said, "One scene really impressed me—the one at the desk." O'Brien's outstanding film career was launched by his giving his all . . . for a part that had seemed worthless!

*Whatsoever thy hand findeth
to do, do it with thy might.*
ECCLESIASTES 9:10

A man once had a friend who was a skilled potter. He often went to watch him at work as he molded the clay into various vessels. One day he asked his friend how he determined what he was going to make. The potter said he had discovered that when he was rested, he tended to make beautiful things, but when he was tired, he made more ordinary vessels for menial uses. As the potter reflected on this, he concluded that when he was relaxed, he had *both the ability to focus and the patience* to make something beautiful. Oftentimes the

Reputation is made in a moment: character is built in a lifetime.

process of making a perfect object involved crushing an almost completed vase or bowl back into a lump so that he might start over. Beautiful objects also required that he be much more careful at each stage. When he was tired, by contrast, he was less able to focus, less patient, and thus more apt to make mistakes and more likely to resort to making items that did not demand such precision.

So it is with our lives. Building character takes focus and patience, with attention to detail and an ability to be consistent over time. While God is ultimately our Potter, we also play the role of potter in forming our own character. The more stressed we are, the less likely we are to create a character of beauty.

My righteousness I hold fast, and
will not let it go: my heart shall
not reproach me so long as I live.
JOB 27:6

> *If you feel "dog tired" at night,*
> *maybe it's because you*
> *"growled" all day.*

General Horace Porter once wrote about a conversation he had with General Ulysses Grant one evening while they were sitting by a campfire. Porter noted, "General, it seems singular that you should have gone through all the rough and tumble of army service and frontier life, and have never been provoked into swearing. I have never heard you utter an oath."

Grant replied, "Well, somehow or other, I never learned to swear. When a boy, I seemed to have an aversion to it, and when I became a man I saw the folly of it. I have always noticed, too, that swearing helps to arouse a man's anger; and when a man flies into a passion his adversary who keeps cool always gets the better of him. In fact, I could never see the value of swearing. I think it is the case with many people who swear excessively that it is a mere habit . . . they do not mean to be profane; to say the least, it is a great waste of time."

Not only does anger give rise to harsh words, but harsh words feed anger. The seething soul uses up valuable inner energy, leaving far less for the normal healthy functioning of spirit, mind, and body. To rid yourself of feelings of anger and frustration, perhaps the first step is to watch your tongue!

If it be possible, as much as lieth in you, live peaceably with all men.

ROMANS 12:18

As college roommates, Meg and Ann also became best friends. Then one day, Meg told Ann that John had asked her for a date. Ann was disappointed; she'd had a crush on John for two years. Still, she managed to say, "Have a good time" and later, to put on a happy face at John and Meg's wedding.

Through the years, Meg kept the relationship with Ann close. Ann enjoyed teasing and laughing with John. When Meg asked Ann to join them at a beachside bungalow for a week, Ann jumped at the chance. On an afternoon when Meg went out to visit a friend, Ann and

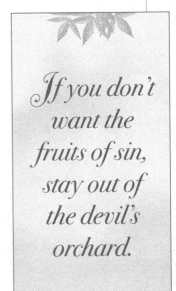

If you don't want the fruits of sin, stay out of the devil's orchard.

John betrayed Meg's trust. Afterward, Ann felt sick inside. Deep shame welled up in her.

A few minutes of flirtation and passion resulted in more than a decade of misery for

Ann. She might never have known happiness again if Meg hadn't confronted her about her refusal to accept a marriage proposal. Ann sobbed, "I'm horrible. You don't know how I've wronged you." Meg said, "I do know, Ann," and one look into her eyes confirmed that Meg had know, had loved, and had forgiven. With that forgiveness, years of shameful pain melted away—pain that could have been avoided by a few right choices easily made at the "beginning" of temptation.

Abstain from all appearances of evil.
1 THESSALONIANS 5:22

> *Our children are like mirrors—they reflect our attitudes in life.*

A man was asked to give a commencement address several years ago and as he sat on the platform after the speech watching the graduates receive their college degrees, the entire audience began applauding for a student who had earned a perfect 4.0 grade point average. During the applause, a faculty member seated next to the speaker leaned over and said to him, "She may be a Genius, but her attitude stinks." The speaker later said, "Without even thinking, my hands stopped clapping for her in mid-air. I couldn't help think, *How sad.*"

No matter how beautiful, intelligent, talented, or athletic a child may be . . . there's no substitute for a child having a positive, loving attitude toward others. The foremost architect of that attitude is not going to be the teacher or a pastor, but the parents.

Be careful in the attitudes you "feed" your children daily. They become the diet of your child's mind, just as food becomes the diet for your child's body. Don't feed your children junk ideas, sour opinions, rotten theology, poisonous feelings, or wilted enthusiasm. Instead, feed your children with the best and most positive ideas, expressions of feeling, and opinions you have.

The just man walketh in his integrity:
his children are blessed after him.

PROVERBS 20:7

A man and his wife once met a young couple about their age during a get-acquainted meeting after church. The next Sunday when they spotted the newcomers again, they invited them to their home for coffee after the Sunday evening service. The newcomers happily accepted their invitation.

Both the conversation and coffee were warm and cozy, but the evening began to grow long. Still, the young couple—perhaps overly eager to make friends—talked on and on about their move to the city, the learning curve they were experi-encing in their new jobs, the difficulty they had settling their children into new schools, their long search for a church home, the trials of finding a dentist, doctor, shoe repairman, and dry cleaning establishment.

The art of being a good guest is knowing when to leave.

No matter how many times the host and hostess yawned or failed to reply, the couple had more to say. Finally, even the visiting couple began to yawn. Still, they made no motion toward leaving.

At long last, the host stood to his feet and with a wide stretch of his arms, he looked at his wife and said, "Well, darlin', let's go up to bed so these nice folks can go home!"

Your chances of being asked back are better when you don't wear out your welcome.

Withdraw thy foot from thy neighbor's house; lest he be weary of thee, and so hate thee.
PROVERBS 25:17

> *He who cannot forgive breaks the bridge over which he himself must pass.*

One Sunday afternoon, Doris Louise Seger opened the door of her church office to practice a violin solo she was to play that night, only to find her violin in pieces, scattered across the floor. Doris was crushed. She had received the violin fifty years earlier as a high school graduation present from her parents. She though, *Who? Why? How can I forgive that person?*

A week later police found the vandal and Doris went to his home. When she saw the skinny, blond 11-year-old sitting next to his father, she understood that the real tragedy was not her shattered violin, but a young life that seemed headed for a shattered future. She explained to the family what the violin had meant to her life and then she found herself saying, "I forgive you, and God will, too, if you ask Him."

A few days later, the boy came to the pastor's office, asking hesitantly, "Is there any work I can do at the church to pay for the violin?" At the sign of his repentant heart, the pastor shared the Gospel with him and the boy received Jesus as his Savior that day.

Doris purchased a new violin, but as she later wrote, "It would never compare with this 'new creature' in Christ Jesus. I learned anew that God's grace is sufficient to give me a forgiving heart."

For if ye forgive men their trespasses, your heavenly Father will also forgive you.
MATTHEW 6:14

Babe Ruth hit 714 home runs during his baseball career, but on this particular day toward the end of his career, the Braves were playing the Reds in Cincinnati, and the great Bambino was no hero. He fumbled the ball and threw badly. In one inning alone, his errors were responsible for most of the five runs scored by Cincinnati.

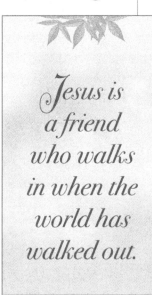

Jesus is a friend who walks in when the world has walked out.

As the Babe walked off the field and headed toward the dugout after the third out, a crescendo of angry cries and boos rose to greet him. Then . . . a boy jumped over the railing and ran out onto the field. With tears streaming down his face, he threw his arms around the legs of his hero.

Ruth didn't hesitate for a second. He picked up the boy, hugged him, then set him down and patted his head. The cries from the crowd abruptly stopped. A hush fell over the entire park. In that brief moment, the fans saw two heroes on the field: Ruth, who, in spite of his own dismal day in fielding, cared about the feelings of a young fan; and a small boy, who cared about the feelings of another human being.

No matter your performance on the playing field of life today, the Lord has a hug awaiting you at the day's end. He is your Number One Fan.

These things I have spoken unto you, that in me ye might have peace. In the world ye shall have tribulation: but be of good cheer; I have overcome the world.
JOHN 16:33

> *Those who deserve love the least need it the most.*

When Mrs. Booth, whose husband founded the Salvation Army, was only a girl, she was running by the road one day with her hoop and stick when she saw a prisoner being dragged by a constable to the city jail. A mob had gathered to hoot at the culprit, who walked with his head hung low—the picture of guilt and shame. His image of utter loneliness tugged at her heart. It seemed to her that he didn't have a friend in the entire world. She quickly sprang to his side and marched, head high and a smile on her face, all the way to the jailhouse with him. She was determined to let him know that, guilty or not, there was at least one soul who felt compassion for him.

Too often we are willing to let guilty people take the full brunt of their punishment, or wallow in their misery, without comfort or words of consolation and encouragement. The issue may not be crime but may be divorce or estrangement. The best way to restore a person to a relationship with both God and the offended party, however, is not to let the person remain alone to become fearful or bitter—but rather, to reach out in love and provide support. This does not mean that you condone the action. It does mean that you refuse to condemn the person!

But I say unto you, Love your enemies, bless them that curse you, do good to them that hate you, and pray for them which despitefully use you, and persecute you.
MATTHEW 5:44

During his two years in the army, David Brenner made the most of his posting in Europe by traveling at every opportunity. To heighten his sense of excitement, he often showed up at a train station and bought a ticket to wherever the next train was going.

One day he bought a ticket for Rome and since the train was scheduled to leave immediately, he raced across the station, but still arrived at the track just as the train was pulling away. He chased after it as fast as he could run! Standing on the platform of the last car

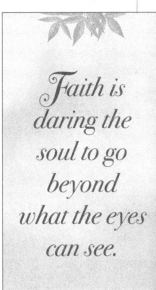

Faith is daring the soul to go beyond what the eyes can see.

was a well-dressed man who motioned for him to hand him his bags. He quickly tossed him his smaller bag and then his larger suitcase. By this time, he was growing weary from running, but then he looked into the man's face! The smirk he was wearing quickly told him that the man had offered his help not altruistically, but criminally. If Brenner didn't make it on board, this man had brand-new clothes and gear!

Brenner kicked up his heels and running as never before, he managed to grab the railing by the entrance to the last car. With all the strength he could muster, he swung himself aboard.

Adversity sometimes comes to rob you. Instead, let it motivate your faith to be even *more* daring!

For we walk by faith, not by sight.
2 CORINTHIANS 5:7

*The right angle to approach
a difficult problem
is the "try-angle."*

Many years ago, a huge oil refinery caught fire. Flames shot hundreds of feet into the air and the sky filled with grimy smoke. The heat was so intense that firefighters parked a block away, hoping for the heat to die down. Instead, the fire raged ever closer to a nearby row of tanks.

Suddenly, a fire truck came careening down the street. With its brakes screeching, it hit the curb directly in front of the blaze. The firefighters jumped out and began to battle the blaze. Inspired by this act, the other firefighters drove closer and joined in the fight. As a result of their cooperative effort, the fire was brought under control in the nick of time.

Those who witnessed these events decided to honor the man who had driven the lead fire truck to the brink of the blaze. In preparing for the awards ceremony, the mayor said, "Captain, we want to honor you for your fantastic act. You prevented the loss of property, perhaps even the loss of life. Is there something we can give you as a token of our appreciation?" The captain replied without hesitation, "Your Honor, a new set of brakes would be dandy!"

Acts of heroism all begin the same way: one person is willing to try when all others are not.

For with God nothing shall be impossible.
LUKE 1:37

For more than a quarter of a century, Arnold Billie was a rural mail carrier in southern New Jersey. His daily route took him sixty-three miles through counties and five municipalities.

Mr. Billie, as he was affectionately known, did more than deliver the mail. He provided "personal service." Anything a person might need to purchase from the post office, Mr. Billie provided—stamps, money orders, pickup service. All a customer needed to do was leave the flag up on their mailbox.

The fellow who does things that count doesn't usually stop to count them.

One elderly woman had trouble starting her lawn mower, so whenever she desired to use it, she would simply leave it by her mailbox, raise the flag, and when Mr. Billie came by, he would start it for her! Mr. Billie gave a new definition to the phrase "public servant."

True Christian servants rarely think of themselves as doing anything other than the ordinary, when what they actually do is quite extraordinary! The apostle Paul called himself a *slave* to Christ, yet he was more concerned about being a good servant to ever worry about being a real slave. Why? Because true servants are motivated by love. It is love they know they have received from Christ. And it is love they give.

Brothers, I do not consider myself yet to have taken hold of it. But one thing I do: Forgetting what is behind and straining toward what is ahead.

PHILIPPIANS 3:13 (NIV)

> *A critical spirit is like poison ivy—it only takes a little contact to spread its poison.*

Glenn Van Ekeren tells about an experience he had with his son one summer vacation. For the first couple of days, his son Matt seemed to misbehave constantly. Glenn seemed to be continually rebuking and correcting him. Thinking, *No son of mine is going to act this way,* he made it clear to his son in no uncertain terms that he expected improved behavior.

Matt tried very hard to live up to his father's standards. In fact, a day went by later in the week in which he hadn't done a single thing that called for correcting. That night, after Matt had said his prayers and jumped into bed, Glenn notice that Matt's bottom lip began to quiver. "What's the matter, buddy?" he asked his son. Barely able to speak, Matt looked up at his father with tear-filled eyes and asked, "Daddy, haven't I been a good boy today?"

Glenn said, "Those words cut through my parental arrogance like a knife. I had been quick to criticize and correct his misbehavior but failed to mention my pleasure with his attempts to be a good boy. My son taught me never to put my children to bed without a word of appreciation and encouragement."

But avoid worldly and empty chatter;
for it will lead to further ungodliness, and
their talk will spread like gangrene.
2 TIMOTHY 2:16,17 (NASB)

One day, a grandfather told his grandchildren about his coming to America. He told of the trains and ship that he took from his home in Eastern Europe. He told of being processed at Ellis Island and how he had gone to a cafeteria in lower Manhattan to get something to eat. There, he sat down at an empty table and waited quite some time for someone to take his order. Nobody came. Finally, a woman with a tray full of food sat down opposite him and explained to him how a cafeteria works.

Laziness and poverty are cousins.

She said, "You start at the end"—pointing toward a stack of trays—"and then go along the food line and pick out what you want. At the other end, they'll tell you how much you have to pay."

The grandfather reflected a moment and then said, "I soon learned that's how everything works in America. Life's a cafeteria here. You can get anything you want—even very great success—if you are willing to pay the price. But you'll never get what you want if you wait for someone to bring it to you. You have to get up and get it yourself."

The difference between where you are and where you want to be can often be summed up in one word: work.

Yet a little sleep, a little slumber, a little folding of the hands to sleep: So shall thy poverty come as one that travelleth; and thy want as an armed man.
PROVERBS 24, 33, 34

> *Language is the expression of thought. Every time you speak your mind is on parade.*

A woman was visiting her brother and his family one time when her nephew suddenly stopped in the midst of his play and steadily gazed up at her. "What are you thinking about?" she asked him. "You're a Christian, auntie, aren't you?" he finally asked.

"I hope so dear," she replied. "But you never talk about Jesus," he said. "If you loved Him *very much,* wouldn't you talk about Him sometimes?"

The aunt, taken aback a bit, stammered a reply: "We may love a person without speaking of him," she said.

"Can we?" her nephew asked innocently. "I didn't know that. You talk about your papa and mamma and your brothers and sisters all the time. And you talk about other people, too—even me. But not Jesus."

"Well, yes," the aunt admitted, her heart quickened with conviction. "I suppose that's been so."

"Let's talk about Jesus sometime," her nephew concluded before getting up to go outside to play. And then, with a backward wink, he added, "'Cause I love Him, too,and I *like* to talk about Him."

We talk about what—and who—matters the most to us. And what we say reveals how we feel about them.

A good man out of the good treasure
of his heart bringeth forth that which
is good; and an evil man out of the evil
treasure of his heart bringeth forth that
which is evil: for of the abundance
of the heart his mouth speaketh.

LUKE 6:45

The first major movie star to wear a uniform in World War II was Jimmy Stewart. Unlike so many other prominent people who sought excuses not to serve, Jimmy willingly accepted the draft and tried to get into the Army Air Corps, since he already had a pilot's license. The corp, however, had a strict weight requirement—for Jimmy's height, a minimum of 153 pounds. Steward weighed 143. When he suggested that they forget to weigh him, the officer responded, "That would be highly irregular." Jimmy replied,

Take care of your character and your reputation will take care of itself.

"Wars are highly irregular, too." With no weighing in, Jimmy won his new role, one in which he prayed often, not for himself, but that "I wouldn't make a mistake."

Stewart worked his way up from buck private to full-fledged pilot, and completed 25 missions over enemy territory, many of them as command pilot of a B-24 bomber wing. By the time he returned to Hollywood he was a full colonel with the Air Medal, Croix de Guerre, Distinguished Flying Cross, and seven battle stars. He remained in the Air Force Reserve and was promoted to Brigadier General in 1959. He once said, "There's a tremendous difference between a warmonger and a patriot." Jimmy Stewart—though a general—was always better known as "the nice guy."

For bodily exercise profiteth little: but godliness is profitable unto all things, having promise of the life that now is, and of that which is to come.

1 TIMOTHY 4:8

A good man leaveth an inheritance to his children's children: and the wealth of the sinner is laid up for the just.

PROVERBS 13:22

The hardest secret for a man to keep is his opinion of himself.

A little Swiss watch had been made with the smallest of parts and great skill. It ran with precision, to the great delight of its owner. Still, the watch was dissatisfied with its restricted sphere of influence on a lady's wrist. It envied the high and lofty position of the great clock on the tower of City Hall.

One day as the little watch and its owner passed City Hall, the tiny watch exclaimed, "I sure wish I could be way up there! I could serve many people instead of just one." The watch's owner looked down and said, "I know someone who has a key to the tower. Little watch, you shall have your opportunity!"

The next day, a slender thread was let down from the tower and the little watch was tied to it. The watch was pulled up the side of the tower—higher and higher it rose! Of course, when it reached the top, it was completely lost to view. "Oh my," said the watch. "My elevation has resulted in my annihilation!"

If you desire to trade your current sphere of small influence for a larger one . . . be wary. The Lord will elevate you in His timing.

For I say, through the grace given unto me, to every man that is among you, not to think of himself more highly than he ought to think; but to think soberly, according as God hath dealt to every man the measure of faith.

ROMANS 12:3

A man named Luigi Tarisio loved violins and began collecting them. He took great pride in scouting out rare finds and purchasing only those instruments that he knew to be of the finest quality. No one really knew about his passion, however, until after he died. It was while his estate was being appraised that some 246 valuable violins were discovered in his attic!

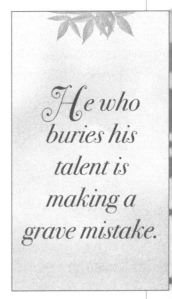

He who buries his talent is making a grave mistake.

One of the most expensive violins had been hidden in the drawer of an old dresser. It was a Stradivarius he had purchased from someone who had also bought it solely as a collector's item. In commenting on this, W. Y. Fullerton noted that in preserving the instrument, Tarisio had robbed the world of beautiful music all the time he treasured his violins. Others before him had done the same. In fact, by the time the greatest Stradivarius violin in his collection was finally played, 147 years had passed!

The gifts, talents, abilities, and aptitudes that you have been given by the Creator are intended for you to discover, and then use until they become perfect. We are to uncover who we were created to be . . . not cover up what we fear we are. Give expression to your inner self today. It is not only God's gift to you, but the very best you can ever give to others.

Neglect not the gift that is in thee.
1 TIMOTHY 4:14

> *If a care is too small to be turned into a prayer, it is too small to be made into a burden.*

Shortly after Mary Manachi's second child, Marylou, was born, she was diagnosed with Cooley's anemia, which requires a blood transfusion every two weeks and is usually fatal before the age of twenty. Assured by physicians that the genetic disorder was very rare, Mary and her husband had another baby. At six months, Rosemarie was also diagnosed with the disorder, and later, her son, George, was also born with Cooley's. Sadness gripped Mary and her husband.

One day, Mary walked into Rosemarie's room and found her making a beautiful pin to sell at a craft show. "I'm going to earn all I can toward college," she said. Then a teacher phoned to report what Rosemarie had written as a thing she was most thankful for: "good health!" Mary took another look at her children and found them *all* embracing life. George was talking about becoming a geologist. Marylou was earning a place on the honor roll and practicing her piano diligently. Mary finally concluded, "If they love life so much . . . am I to love life less?"

Sometimes our burdens seem great. It helps at those times to remember those with great burdens who carry them as "being too small" even to become worries.

Casting all your care upon him; for he careth for you.
1 PETER 5:7

A woman was sitting in her den one day when a small black snake suddenly appeared, slithered across the floor, and made its way under the couch. Being deathly afraid of snakes, the woman promptly ran to the bathroom to get her husband, who was taking a shower. He came running from the shower with only a towel around his waist, grabbed an old broom handle from the closet, and began poking under the couch.

At this point, the sleeping family dog awoke. Curious to see what was happening, he

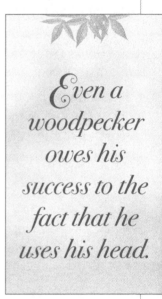

Even a woodpecker owes his success to the fact that he uses his head.

came up behind the husband and touched his cold nose to the back of the man's heel. The man, surmising that the snake had outmaneuvered him and had bitten him on the heel, fainted dead away. The wife concluded that her husband had overexerted and collapsed with a heart attack. She ran from the house to a hospital just one block away. The ambulance drivers promptly returned with her to the house and placed the man on the stretcher. As they were carrying him out of the house, the snake reappeared beneath the couch. One of the drivers became so excited that he dropped his end of the stretcher and broke the husband's leg. Seeing her husband's twisted leg, the wife collapsed.

Meanwhile, the snake slithered quietly away!

But you, keep your head in all situations.
2 Timothy 4:5 (NIV)

> *The poorest of all men is not the man without a cent but the man without a dream.*

An unusual band of thirteen business professional men in Toronto, Canada, respond in a unique way to multiple-alarm fires in their city. They have formed a volunteer firefighting unit, although they don't directly fight fires. Dressed in their own rubber firefighting uniforms, they are armed with police passes. The truck they man is a red mobile canteen.

The firefighters appreciate their service—in fact, the firefighters union bought the canteen truck for them, and also purchased all supplies for the truck. When a fire alarm is received, a "must" call goes to them.

These firefighters describe themselves as "middle-aged businessmen who never outgrew their childhood dreams."

What is it that you dreamed of doing as a child?

In the most reflective moments of your life, do you still nurture that dream? Do you wonder "what might have been if . . . ?"

Dreams are not only a great source of hope and courage, they are often windows to one's destiny. Revisit your childhood dreams. Perhaps it's time for you to give them expression.

Where there is no vision, the people perish.
PROVERBS 29:18

Rachel and Jim owned a commercial building, half of which Jim used for his dental practice. For fifteen years, they had experienced no difficulty in renting out the other half. They counted on the extra money to pay their bills. Then they lost their renter. A real estate agent told them, "Forget about advertising for awhile. Absolutely nobody is renting."

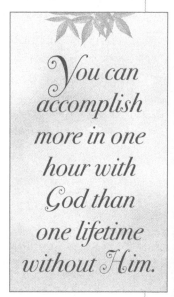

You can accomplish more in one hour with God than one lifetime without Him.

To ease her financial worries, Rachel started swimming laps at her local YMCA pool. One day when she was feeling especially anxious, she decided to pray as she swam, using the alphabet to keep track of the number of laps. She focused on adjectives to describe God, starting with the letter A. You are the *almighty* God," she prayed on lap one. "A *benevolent* God, a *beautiful* God," she prayed on the next lap, and then, "You are a *caring, creative, can-do* God." By the time she had completed 26 laps, an hour had passed and her fears were gone. She *knew* God would provide.

A short time later, a physical therapist called to say she had seen the "For Rent" sign in the window and asked to see the office. It was what she wanted. So, she and her partner rented the space. Rachel still prays while swimming laps. "After all," she says, "I've discovered God's goodness stretches from A to Z!"

With God all things are possible.
MATTHEW 19:26

> *The only preparation for tomorrow is the right use of today.*

A comic strip created by Charles Schulz addresses the need for each of us to make the most of the immediate present in our lives:

Charlie Brown is seen at bat. STRIKE THREE. He has struck out again and slumps down on the player's bench. He says, "Rats! I'll never be a big-league player. I just don't have it! All my life I've dreamed of playing in the big leagues, but I know I'll never make it!"

Lucy turns to console him. "Charlie Brown," she says, "you're thinking too far ahead. What you need to do is set yourself more immediate goals."

Charlie Brown looks up and asks, "Immediate goals?" Lucy responds, "Yes. Start with this next inning when you go out to pitch. See if you can walk to the mound without falling down."

The first step toward walking into any future is the step that you take today. Make it a forward . . . positive . . . springy and lighthearted . . . energetic . . . well-aimed . . . purposeful step. The steps you take today become the well-worn path of tomorrow.

*Take therefore no thought for the morrow:
for the morrow shall take thought
for the things of itself. Sufficient
unto the day is the evil thereof.*
MATTHEW 6:34

Medical missionary Dr. Lambie, formerly of Abyssinia, forded many swift and bridgeless streams in Africa. He learned from the natives the best way to make a hazardous crossing.

The danger in crossing a stream lies in being swept off one's feet and carried downstream to deeper waters or being hurled to death against hidden rocks. A way to avoid this is for a man about to cross a stream to find a large stone, the heavier the better, to lift it to his shoulder, and carry it across the stream as a ballast. The extra weight of the stone keeps his feet solid on the bed of the stream.

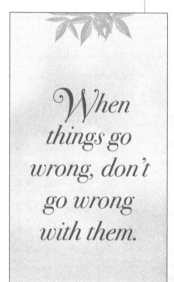

When things go wrong, don't go wrong with them.

In telling of this technique, Dr. Lambie drew an application to life: "While crossing the dangerous stream of life . . . we need the ballast of burden-bearing . . . to keep us from being swept off our feet."

This does not mean that we should seek out troubles or give in to our problems. Rather, it means that as we look around at others, we are to help shoulder their burdens and in return, to accept their help in bearing our own loads. It's easy to become overwhelmed in carrying only your own burden. Shared burdens, however, "travel lighter."

Enter not into the path of the wicked,
and go not in the way of evil men.

PROVERBS 4:14

> *Two things are hard on the heart—running upstairs and running down people.*

A faculty member at a university once became very distraught over the weaknesses of a particular administrator with whom he had a negative relationship. He allowed himself to think about the man constantly. Hateful, negative thoughts so preoccupied him that it affected the quality of his relationships with his family, his church, and his colleagues. He finally concluded that he needed to leave and accept a teaching appointment elsewhere.

A friend asked him, "Wouldn't you really prefer to teach at this university, if the man were not here?" "Of course," the man responded, "but as long as he is here, then my staying is too disruptive to everything in life. I have to go."

The friend then asked, "Why have you made this administrator the center of your life?" As much as the man tried to deny the truth of this, he finally had to admit that he had allowed one individual and his weaknesses to distort his entire view of life. Still, it was not the administrator's doing. It was his own. From that day forward, he focused on his students and his teaching . . . and he found new joy in his "old job."

When you concentrate on running down others, usually the only one that gets run down is you.

Let no corrupt communication proceed out of your mouth, but that which is good to the use of edifying, that it may minister grace unto the hearers.

EPHESIANS 4:29

In his book, *Beneath the Cross of Jesus,* A. Leonard Griffith tells the story of a young Korean exchange student, a leader in Christian circles at the University of Pennsylvania, who left his apartment on the evening of April 25, 1958, to mail a letter to his parents. As he turned from the mailbox, he was met by eleven leather-jacketed teenage boys. Without a word, they beat him with a blackjack, a lead pipe, and their shoes and fists—and left him lying dead in the gutter.

The best way to get even is to forget.

All Philadelphia cried out for vengeance. The district attorney planned to seek the death penalty for the arrested youth. And then, this letter arrived, signed by the boy's parents and twenty other relatives in Korea: "Our family has met together and we have decided to petition that the most generous treatment possible within the laws of your government be given to those who have committed this criminal action . . . . In order to give evidence of our sincere hope contained in this petition, we have decided to save money to start a fund to be used for the religious, educational, vocational, and social guidance of the boys when they are released . . . . We have dared to express our hope with a spirit received from the gospel of our Savior Jesus Christ who died for our sins."

When you forgive it takes you from the place of the victim to that of the victor.

But love your enemies, and do good, and lend, hoping for nothing again; and your reward shall be great, and ye shall be the children of the Highest: for he is kind unto the unthankful and to the evil.

LUKE 6:35

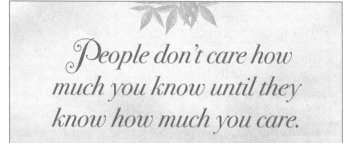

People don't care how much you know until they know how much you care.

Although the North American Indians had no written alphabet before they met the white man, their language was anything but primitive. The vocabulary of many Indian languages was as large as that of their French and English conquerors. Often, their expressions were far more eloquent. In an Indian tongue, for example, the concept for the word *friend* is beautifully stated as "one-who-carried-my-sorrows-on-his-back."

A friend or family member who comes to you for solace . . . or even claiming to be seeking advice . . . very often wants nothing more than your presence, your listening ear, and your quiet caring of sorrows. A young man discovered this shortly after his marriage. His wife frequently came home from her job telling of the woes of her day. His response was to offer suggestions and give solutions. His wife finally said to him, "I've already solved the problems of the day." The husband asked, perplexed, "Then why are you telling me about them?" She replied, "I don't need Mr. Fixit. I need a loving ear."

The friend who provides both physical and emotional shelter is a true haven. A friend is one who helps another weather a storm in safety.

Let nothing be done through strife or vainglory; but in lowliness of mind let each esteem others better than themselves.

PHILIPPIANS 2:3

Standup comedian and author David Brenner was signing books in a San Francisco bookstore when a young man handed him a newly purchased copy to be signed and said softly, "I want to thank you for saving my life." Brenner replied flippantly, "That's okay." The young many stood his ground and said, "No, I really mean it."

Brenner stopped signing and looked at him. The man said, "My father died. He was my best friend. I loved him and couldn't stop crying for weeks. I decided to take my own life. The

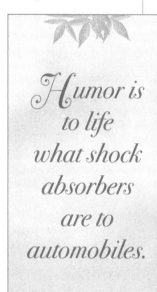

Humor is to life what shock absorbers are to automobiles.

night I was going to do it, I happened to have the TV on. You were hosting *The Tonight Show,* doing your monologue. Next thing I knew I was watching you and laughing. Then I started laughing hysterically. I realized then that if I was able to laugh, I was able to live. So I want to thank you for saving my life." Humbled and grateful, Brenner shook his hand and said, "No, I thank you."

Laughter does more than help us escape our problems. It sometimes gives us the courage to face them. As humorous author Barbara Johnson has said, "Laughter is like changing a baby's diaper. It doesn't permanently solve any problems, but it makes things more acceptable for awhile."

A merry heart doeth good like a medicine: but a broken spirit drieth the bones.

PROVERBS 17:22

> *A* man wrapped up
> in himself makes a
> very small package.

A pompous city man, turned farmer, was showing a young boy over his acreage. As they drove through field after field, the man bragged incessantly about his accomplishments—how he had started from scratch as a young man and worked his way up through the business world. He told how he had earned far more money than had been necessary to purchase the land and how he had invested thousands upon thousands of dollars to transform the formerly worthless farm into the agricultural paradise they were surveying. He told of the amazing yield of his crops, and the lushness of the new spring planting.

Finally, he pointed toward the stacked hay, the full granary, and the boxes of produce and declared, "And I grew it all by myself, sonny. Started with nothing, and now look at it!"

"From nothing?" echoed the duly impressed lad.

"That's right," said the man. "From nothing."

"Wow," the young boy said, pausing to reflect for a few seconds. "My dad farms, but he needs seed to grow his crops."

A fool finds no pleasure in understanding but delights in airing his own opinions.
PROVERBS 18:2 (NIV)

A traditional Supervisor's Prayer states: Lord, when I am wrong, make me willing to change. When I am right, make me easy to live with. So strengthen me that the power of my example will far exceed the authority of my rank.

A positive attitude may not directly change your circumstances, but it *will* change the way you respond to your circumstances. The responses of positive people are far more likely to be:

- active
- solution oriented
- generous towards others
- involving of others
- immediate or timely
- rooted in dignity and respect

It isn't your position that makes you happy or unhappy, it's your disposition.

Positive people are much more likely than are negative people to turn their ideas into positive behavior. Positive behavior, in turn, *does* change circumstances, and nearly always so, for the better.

Truly to grab hold of a slippery problem and rise above it, first grab hold of a positive thought.

But godliness with contentment is great gain.
For we brought nothing into this world,
and it is certain we can carry nothing out.
1 TIMOTHY 6:6,7

> *It takes more to plow a field
> than merely turning it
> over in your mind.*

An author, a cynical man, once sought to escape city life by moving to a little house in the country. His house was located across the street from a farm, and from his library window, he often looked up from his writing to watch as his neighbor engaged in a wide variety of jobs that needed to be done on his farm. He was intrigued to the point of distraction.

He watched as the man mended the fence after his cattle had broken through it. He watched as the man replanted a field after a heavy deluge washed out a new planting. He watched as he made repairs to his tractor and removed several large stones from his field after a tractor blade broke. The farmer seemed to work from sunup to sundown, doing battle against the elements and facing one problem after another with unlimited energy. The author began to wonder about the man's optimism.

One day the author strolled from his cottage to talk to the farmer, "You amaze me," he said after he greeted his neighbor. "You never seem to lose heart. Do you *always* hope for the best?"

The farmer thought for a moment and then with eyes flashing, he replied, "No, I don't hope for it—I *hop* for it!"

Work with your hands, just as
we commanded you, so that
you may behave properly toward
outsiders and not be in any need.
1 THESSALONIANS 4:11,12 (NASB)

Abraham Lincoln is often held up to children as a model of achievement and an embodiment of "The American Dream." Regarded by many as the greatest President of the United States, Lincoln's Second Inaugural Address is one of the noblest political speeches ever given, and his Gettysburg Address is still studied and memorized by many a student. Amazingly, Lincoln had only four months of formal education, and that in a one-room country schoolhouse where students ranged from age five to twenty-five. His teacher probably

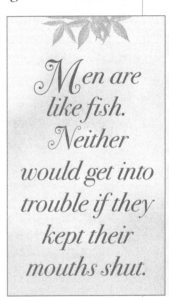

Men are like fish. Neither would get into trouble if they kept their mouths shut.

had no more than an eighth-grade education, if that.

One day a father was reciting all of these achievements to his son. "Where else but in

America could this happen?" he mused. And then, hoping to instill in his son a little more ambition to study, he asked, "Do you know what Abe Lincoln was doing when he was your age?"

The boy answered, "No, but I do know what he was doing when he was your age."

We nearly always err when we suggest to others they be like anybody other than their own best selves. And, to our chagrin, they usually let us know we have erred.

Whoso keepeth his mouth and his tongue keepeth his soul from troubles.
PROVERBS 21:23

The heart of a man cannot be determined by the size of his pocketbook.

Not a lot of press coverage was given to the tough Argentine golfer Robert De Vincenzo, but one story from his life shows his greatness as a person.

After winning a tournament, De Vincenzo received his check on the eighteenth green, flashed a smile for the cameras, and then walked alone to the clubhouse. As he went to his car, he was approached by a sad-eyed young woman who said to him, "It's a good day for you, but I have a baby with an incurable disease. It's of the blood, and the doctors say she will die." De Vincenzo paused and then asked, "May I help your little girl?" He then took out a pen, endorsed his winning check, and then pressed it into her hand. "Make some good days for the baby," he said.

A week later as he was having lunch at a country club, a PGA official approached him saying, "Some of the boys in the parking lot told me you met a young woman after you won the tournament." De Vincenzo nodded. The official said, "Well, she's a phony. She has no sick baby. She fleeced you, my friend."

The golfer looked up and asked, "You mean that there is no baby who is dying without hope?" This time the PGA official nodded. De Vincenzo grinned and said, "that's the best news I've heard all week."

For what shall it profit a man, if he shall gain the whole world, and lose his own soul? Or what shall a man give in exchange for his soul?
MARK 8:36,37

After two years of marriage, Peter no longer saw his wife as interesting, fun, or attractive. In his mind, he regarded her as a sloppy housekeeper, overweight, and a woman with a fault-finding personality. He sought out a divorce attorney, who advised him: "Pete, if you really want to get even with your wife, start treating her like a *queen!* Do everything in your power to serve her, please her, and make her feel special. Then, after a couple of months of this royal treatment, pack your bags and leave. That way you'll disappoint her as much as she has disappointed you." Pete could hardly wait to enact the plan! He picked up a dozen roses on his way home, helped his wife with the dinner dishes, brought her breakfast in bed, and began complimenting

Kindness is the oil that takes the friction out of life.

her on her clothes, cooking, and housekeeping. He treated her to an out-of-town trip.

After three months, the attorney called and said, "Well, I have the divorce papers ready for you to sign. In a matter of minutes, you can be a happy bachelor."

"Are you crazy?" Pete said. "My wife has made so many changes. I wouldn't think of divorcing her now."

Kindness extended toward another person may not change the other person, but it does change the person showing kindness . . . it makes them kinder.

But the fruit of the spirit is . . . kindness.
GALATIANS 5:22 (NIV)

GLDB

> *You can easily determine the caliber of a person by the amount of opposition it takes to discourage him.*

A student found a cocoon one day and brought it to his biology teacher. She put it in a glass box with a warming lamp. About a week later, the students saw a small opening appear on the cocoon. Then, the cocoon began to shake. Suddenly, tiny antennae emerged, followed by a head and tiny front feet. The students watched the progress of the emerging insect throughout the day. By noon it had freed its listless wings, the colors revealing it to be a monarch butterfly. It wiggled and shook, but try as it might, it could not seem to force its body through the small opening. One student decided to snip off the end of the cocoon to help the insect. Out it plopped. Only the top half of it looked like a butterfly, however. The bottom half was large and swollen. The insect crawled about, dragging its listless wings, and a short time later, it died.

The next day, the biology teacher explained that the butterfly's struggle to get through the tiny opening is necessary in order to force fluids from its swollen body into the wings so they will be strong enough to fly. Without the struggle, the wings never develop.

Struggles cause numerous things in our lives to develop. Rather than struggle *against* struggle, we need to struggle *through* our struggles!

If thou faint in the day of adversity, thy strength is small.
PROVERBS 24:10

While doing research for a doctoral thesis, a young man spent a year with a group of Navajo Indians on a reservation in the Southwest. He lived with one family, sleeping in their hut, eating their food, working with them, and generally living their life.

The grandmother of the family spoke no English, yet a very close relationship formed between the grandmother and the doctoral student. They seemed to share the common language of love and they intuitively understood each other. Over the months he learned a few phrases of Navajo, and she picked up words and phrases in English.

People know what you are by what they see, not by what they hear.

When it was time for the young man to return to the university to write his thesis, the tribe held a going-away celebration for him. It was marked by sadness since he had developed a close relationship with all those in the village. As he prepared to get into his pickup truck and drive away, the old grandmother came to tell him goodbye. With tears streaming from her eyes, she placed her hands on either side of his face, looked directly into his eyes, and said, "I like me best when I'm with you."

True friendship is letting those around you not only "be themselves" but "be their best."

Let your light so shine before men,
that they may see your good works, and
glorify your Father which is in heaven.
MATTHEW 5:16

> *People who try to whittle you down are only trying to reduce you to their size.*

Japanese bonsai trees are tiny, perfectly formed specimens. Their stature remains small no matter how old a tree gets—most bonsai trees being only fifteen to eighteen inches tall. To make a bonsai tree, a young sapling is first pulled from the soil. Then, its taproot and some of the feeder roots are tied off. Thus the growth of the bonsai tree is deliberately stunted.

In sharp contrast, the California sequoia trees grow large. The General Sherman stands 272 feet and measures 79 feet in circumference. If felled, this giant tree would provide enough lumber to build 35 five-room homes! The sequoia begins life as a small seed, no larger than the bonsai seed. But its sapling is allowed to be nourished in the rich California soil and sunshine.

Neither the bonsai nor the giant sequoia has a choice in determining how large it will become. But we human beings do! We cannot blame others—including our parents—for what they have done or are doing to us. We have the potential to transplant ourselves into rich, nurturing positive environments.

If others are trying to whittle you down today, get away from their knife! Rejoice in who you are and who you can be. Find a new place to put down roots.

Blessed are ye, when men shall hate you, and when they shall separate you from their company, and shall reproach you, and cast out your name as evil, for the Son of man's sake. Rejoice ye in that day, and leap for joy: for, behold, your reward is great in heaven.

LUKE 6:22, 23

A mother was helping her son one day with his spelling assignment and they came to the words *conscious* and *conscience*. She asked her son, "Do you know the difference between these two words?"

He immediately replied, "Sure, Mom. Conscious is when you are aware of something. And, con-science is when you wish you weren't."

The conscience is like a sharp square peg in our hearts. When we are confronted by a situation that calls for a right-or-wrong decision, that square begins to turn. Its

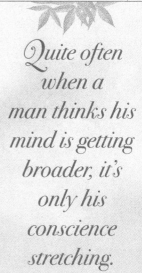

Quite often when a man thinks his mind is getting broader, it's only his conscience stretching.

corner cuts into our hearts, warning us with an inward "knowing" that we are facing a situation in which we must make a choice against evil and for good.

If the conscience is ignored time after time, however, the corners of the square are gradually worn down and it becomes a circle that twists and turns at will. When that circle turns within our hearts, there is no inner sensation of warning. In effect, we are left without a conscience.

A sound conscience is truly a gift from God. Heed its warning signals early and you will be spared much pain and heartache.

Unto the pure all things are pure:
but unto them that are defiled and
unbelieving is nothing pure; but even
their mind and conscience is defiled.

TITUS 1:15

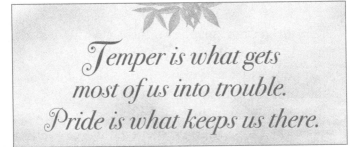

> *Temper is what gets
> most of us into trouble.
> Pride is what keeps us there.*

In an old monastery near Bebenhausen, Germany, one may see two pairs of deer horns hanging on the wall. The horns are interlocked.

They were found in that position many years ago. Apparently two bucks had been fighting for territorial or herd rights, and their horns became jammed together and could not be separated. They died in a fighting position, unable to find a way of cooperating so that on bended knees, both might eat or drink or eventually free itself from the other.

These locked horns are not unlike many relationships that can be found today in homes, schools, factories, offices, and even churches. People become entrenched in their positions and angrily confront those who oppose them. In the process, they "lock horns" and seem unable to ask each other for forgiveness, or to find a mutual way of serving one another in love. Both parties in such a relationship suffer, and ultimately lose.

If you are at odds with someone today, go to that person and ask what the two of you might do to reconcile. You may be surprised to find that the other person wants reconciliation as much as you do.

Pride goeth before destruction, and a haughty spirit before a fall. Better it is to be of a humble spirit with the lowly, than to divide the spoil with the proud.
PROVERBS 16:18,19

Two brothers farmed together. They lived in separate houses on the family farm, but met each day in the fields to work together. One brother married and had a large family. The other lived alone. Still, they divided the harvest from the fields equally.

One night the single brother thought, *My brother is struggling to support a large family, but I get half of the harvest*. With love in his heart, he gathered a box of things he had purchased from his earnings—items he knew would help his brother's family. He planned to slip over to his brother's shed, unload the basket there, and never say a word about it.

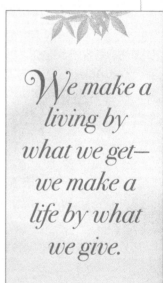

We make a living by what we get— we make a life by what we give.

That same night, the married brother thought, *My brother is alone. He doesn't know the joys of a family*. Out of love, he decided to take over a basket with a quilt and homemade bread and preserves to "warm" his brother's house. He planned to leave the items on his porch and never say a word.

As the brothers stealthily made their way toward each other's home, they bumped into one another. They were forced to admit to what they were doing and there in the darkness, they cried and embraced, each man realizing that his greatest wealth was a brother who respected and loved him.

I have showed you all things, how
that so laboring ye ought to support the
weak, and to remember the words of the
Lord Jesus, how he said, It is more
blessed to give than to receive.

ACTS 20:35

*Our days are identical suitcases—
all the same size—but some
people can pack more
into them than others.*

Sparky didn't have much going for him. He failed every subject in the eighth grade, and in high school, he flunked Latin, algebra, English, and physics. He made the golf team, but promptly lost the only important match of the season, and then lost the consolation match. He was awkward socially—more shy than disliked. He never once asked a girl to go out on a date in high school.

One thing, however, was important to Sparky—drawing. He was proud of his artwork even though no one else appreciated it. He submitted cartoons to the editors of his high school yearbook, but they were turned down. Even so, Sparky aspired to be an artist. After high school, he sent samples of his artwork to the Walt Disney Studios. Again, he was turned down.

Still, Sparky didn't quit packing his suitcase! He decided to write his own autobiography in cartoons. The subject not only of cartoon strips but countless books, television shows, and licensing opportunities. Sparky, you see, was Charles Schulz, creator of the "Peanuts" comic strip. Like his character, Charlie Brown, Schulz may not have been able to do many things. But, he made the most of what he *could* do.

Be very careful, then, how you live—
not as unwise but as wise, making
the most of every opportunity.
Ephesians 5:15,16 (niv)

Firmin Abautiz was known as a man of serene disposition. Nobody in his town could recall his having lost his temper at any time during his 87 years. One man, who doubted the possibility that a person could be so unflappable, made a deal with a housekeeper, offering her money if she could provoke him to anger.

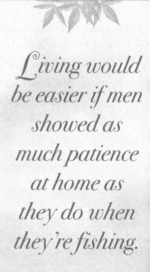

Living would be easier if men showed as much patience at home as they do when they're fishing.

The housekeeper knew that Abautiz was very fond of a comfortable, orderly, bed, so she neglected to make his bed one day. The next morning, Abautiz kindly reminded her of the undone chore. The next night, Abautiz again found an unmade bed and the following morning, he again called it to her attention. She made a lame excuse, which he kindly accepted.

On the third morning, Abautiz said, "You still have not made my bed; it is evident you are determined not to do it. Well, I suppose you find the job troublesome, but it is of little consequence, for I begin to be used to it already." Moved by such goodness of temper, the woman called off the deal and never again failed to make his bed as comfortable as possible!

Not everything can be the way we like it all the time, but criticism and harsh words rarely bring about a lasting and peaceful cooperation or fulfillment of our desires. Patience and kindness, on the other hand, do.

You husbands, likewise, live with your wives in an understanding way.

1 PETER 3:7 (NASB)

> *Some people succeed because
> they are destined to, but
> most people succeed because
> they are determined to.*

There once was a Louisville University quarterback who dreamed of playing pro football. Upon graduation, however, no pro team drafted him. So, he wrote to several teams and finally got an opportunity to try out for the Pittsburgh Steelers. He gave his best effort, but wasn't chosen. His friends said, "You got a raw deal . . . it wasn't meant to be . . . I guess it's time to hang up your cleats." But the young athlete didn't give up. He continued to knock on doors and write letters. Finally, he received another invitation. But again, he didn't make the team.

Most people would have given up long before this point, but not Johnny. He was fanatic about his personal dream. From his early days of playing sandlot football, he had been obsessed with this goal. So, patiently and persistently, he continued to pursue try-out opportunities. Finally, he was invited to try out for the Baltimore team . . . and he made the third string! Through training and long man-hours of drills and fitness building, he worked his way up to be starting quarterback. Indeed, he became one of the greatest quarterbacks ever to play in the NFL. The dreamer's name was Johnny Unitas.

Keep driving until you arrive at your goal line!

Having done all to stand, stand.
EPHESIANS 6:13,14

There once was a saintly man who lived on the edge of poverty . . . by his own choice. The money he earned, he distributed equally between himself and the poor. The man's adult son was among those who found it extremely difficult to make ends meet, so the man gave him just enough to keep body and soul together, even as he continued to help others who found themselves in dire need. One day the father was asked why he paid so little attention to his son's personal needs, while the bulk of his attention went to others. "You could help your son much more," his critic said, "if you would help strangers less."

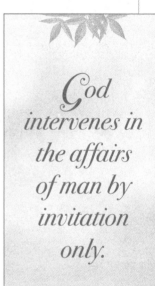

God intervenes in the affairs of man by invitation only.

"Ah," the man replied wisely, "but if I were to meet all my son's requirements, would he perhaps forget the necessity of relying upon the Lord? Would he begin to see me as the source of all his supply, rather than his Heavenly Father? If that became the case, I would not be helping my son at all."

God forbid that we find ourselves feeling totally self-sufficient, without need. It is in that dark corner that pride lurks. Once pride takes over, we see little reason to invite the Lord to do *His* work in our lives. Take inventory. Have you invited God into the affairs of your life lately?

Behold, I stand at the door, and knock: if any man hear my voice, and open the door, I will come in to him, and will sup with him, and he with me.

REVELATION 3:20

The difference between ordinary and extraordinary is that little extra.

Charles F. Kettering, a noted scientist and inventor, believed that the easiest way to overcome defeat was simply to ignore the possibility of failure and to keep forging ahead. He once gave an address to Denison University on this theme. He told how he had once given a tough project assignment to a young research worker in a laboratory at General Motors. He wanted to see how the man would react to a difficult problem so he kept from him notes about the project that had been filed in the lab's library. These notes, written by expert researchers, included various sets of statistics and formulas that proved the assignment the young man had been given was impossible to do.

The young research worker set his mind to the project, and worked virtually night and day for weeks. He refused to give up or think the project impossible. One day he came confidently to Kettering to show his work. He had succeeded in doing the impossible!

A little extra time . . . a little extra effort . . . a little extra care . . . a little extra attention sometimes makes all the difference between success and failure, and not only that, but the difference between good and great.

Whatsoever thy hand findeth to do, do it with thy might; for there is no work, nor device, nor knowledge, nor wisdom, in the grave, whither thou goest.
ECCLESIASTES 9:10

A small-town newspaper developed a column specifically to interview couples in the town who had reached their Golden Anniversary of marriage. A brief history of the couple celebrating fifty years of marriage was outlined. Then, the newspaper posed the same question to each spouse: "To what do you attribute the success of your marriage?" Many of the couples approaching this milestone knew they were going to be interviewed and they gave long thought to the wisest and most practical advice they could give. Some advocated total honesty, others a shared faith, and others abundant communication.

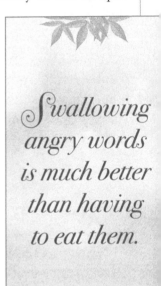

Swallowing angry words is much better than having to eat them.

One man lovingly glanced at his wife and then replied: "The secret of our fifty years of marital harmony is quite simple. My wife and

I made an agreement the day we were married. If she was bothered or upset about something, she was to get it off her chest and out in the open. We felt it was important for her to get it out of her system. And, if I was made at her about something, we agreed I would take a walk. So, I guess you can attribute our marital success to the fact that I have led largely an outdoor life."

In finding a way to release anger and frustration, make sure your loved ones aren't part of your method.

A fool uttereth all his mind: but a wise man keepeth it in till afterwards.

PROVERBS 29:11

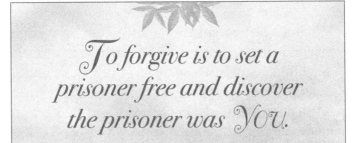

*To forgive is to set a
prisoner free and discover
the prisoner was you.*

On February 9, 1960, Adolph Coors III was kidnapped and held for ransom. His body was found seven months later on a remote hillside. He had been shot to death. Adolph Coors IV, who was fifteen years old at the time, lost not only his father but his best friend. For years, young Coors hated Joseph Corbett, the man who was sentenced to life for the slaying.

Then in 1975 Adolph Coors became a Christian. He knew this hatred for Corbett blinded his growth in faith and also alienated him from other people. Still, resentment seethed within him. He prayed, asking God to help him stop hating Corbett.

Coors eventually felt led to visit Corbett in the maximum security unit of Colorado's

Canon City penitentiary. Corbett refused to see him, but Coors left a Bible with this inscription: "I'm here to see you today and I'm sorry that we could not meet. As a Christian I am summoned by our Lord and Savior, Jesus Christ, to forgive. I do forgive you, and I ask you to forgive me for the hatred I've held in my heart for you." Coors later confessed, "I have a love for that man that only Jesus Christ could have put in my heart." Coors' heart, imprisoned by hatred, was at last set free.

For if ye forgive men their trespasses, your heavenly Father will also forgive you: But if ye forgive not men their trespasses, neither will your Father forgive your trespasses.

MATTHEW 6:14,15

Have you ever seen an entire oyster shell without an oyster in it? You may have wondered, *How did the oyster get out?* You might look for a very small hole in the top of the shell. Such a hole is made by a whelk. This little ocean creature has an appendage that works somewhat like an auger. With it, the whelk bores into the oyster shell and then sucks the oyster through the hole, little by little, until it has devoured it all. Though small, a whelk can do great harm!

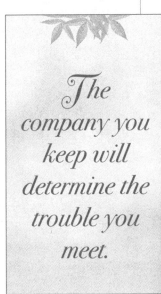

The company you keep will determine the trouble you meet.

Very often, we allow another person's angry outbursts, their critical remarks, or their cynical comments to bore a hole into our good nature and rob us of our otherwise sunny disposition. If we aren't careful, we can become irritated to the point where genuine anger and bitterness begin to seethe in us. And when that happens, we are in very real danger of experiencing disease, disharmony, and discord.

One of the best things you can do is simply to avoid those people whom you find irksome, continually critical, or habitually angry at life, as well as those who seem to delight in needling you. In other words, stay out of the way of whelks. You'll be healthier and happier for it!

Make no friendship with an angry man;
and with a furious man thou shalt
not go: Lest thou learn his ways,
and get a snare to thy soul.
PROVERBS 22:24,25

GLDB

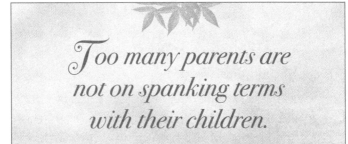

> *Too many parents are
> not on spanking terms
> with their children.*

A boy once made headlines as the result of his repeated vandalism in his neighborhood. Even though he came from a well-to-do family, he was, by every indication of behavior, a perfect example of a "juvenile delinquent." A reporter quizzed the boy in detention, asking, "Why do you feel the need to destroy property? Are you angry?" The boy just shrugged his shoulders and turned away. The reporter persisted, "Weren't you afraid of getting a licking from your parents?"

At this the boy looked at the reporter, and said, "I've never had a licking in my life." The tone of his voice however, was not one of anger, but of sadness. The reporter talked with him further and realized that "not having a licking" meant to this young boy that his parents didn't care one whit about him. The young man concluded the interview by declaring that if the police turned him loose, he would continue to take out his vengeance on the neighborhood until one or the other of his folks cared enough to stop him.

Spanking is not abuse. Abuse is rooted in a parent's uncontrolled expression of power. Spanking is a form of discipline intended to restrain and rechannel a child's uncontrolled expression of power! Abuse never has a place. Spanking sometimes does.

He who spares his rod hates
his son, But he who loves him
disciplines him diligently.
PROVERBS 13:24 (NASB)

Centuries ago, when a mapmaker would run out of the known world before he ran out of parchment, he often would sketch a dragon at the edge of the scroll. This was intended to be a sign to the explorer that he was entering unknown territory at his own risk.

Many explorers, however, did not perceive the dragon as a mapmaker's warning sign, but rather, as a prophecy. They foresaw disaster and doom beyond the "known worlds" they traversed. Their fear kept them from pushing on to discover new lands and peoples.

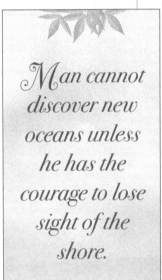

Man cannot discover new oceans unless he has the courage to lose sight of the shore.

Other more adventuresome travelers saw the dragon as a sign of opportunity, the doorway to a new territory worth exploring.

Each of us has a mental map that contains the information we use for guidance as we explore each new day. Like the maps of long ago, our mental maps have edges to them, and sometimes those edges seem to be marked by dragons, or fears. At times, our fears may be valid. But at other times, our fears may keep us from discovering more of this world, or more about other people—including ourselves. Don't let fear keep you from all that God desires for you to explore and to know.

And Peter answered him and said, Lord,
if it be thou, bid me come unto thee
on the water. And he said, Come. And
when Peter was come down out of the ship,
he walked on the water, to go to Jesus.
MATTHEW 14:28,29

> *The heart is the happiest when it beats for others.*

One of the people most admired by Charles Swindoll is Dawson Trotman, who died after helping to rescue two drowning girls. Says Swindoll:

"When Dawson Trotman passed away he probably left a legacy of discipleship on this earth that will never be matched except perhaps in the life of Jesus Christ Himself. I've become a real student of Dawson Trotman and believe wholeheartedly in the methods of discipleship that he taught and emulated throughout his days. He died in Schroon Lake, New York. He died of all things in the midst of an area that he was expert in—he drowned. He was an expert swimmer. The last few moments he had in the water, he lifted one girl out of the water. He went down and got the other girl and then lifted her out of the water and then submerged and was not found again until the dragnet found him a few hours later. . . . *Time* ran an article on Trotman's life the next week, and they put a caption beneath his name and it read, 'Always Holding Somebody Up.' In one sentence, that was Trotman's life— investment in people . . . holding them up."

Discipleship is not having others follow you as much as it is lifting others up to see the Lord and then serving them so they can follow Him wholeheartedly.

Greater love hath no man than this, that a man lay down his life for his friends.
JOHN 15:13

A man was once drawn by the idea that living in "quiet contemplation away from human society" was the sure path to happiness. He wandered into the desert to become a hermit. After many days, he found a cave near a spring where he could obtain water and grow a few plants for food. Feeling self-sufficient, he spent many idle hours in solitude. Eventually, the hours of the day seemed never to end. His loneliness oppressed him. Feeling more wretched than holy, he cried, "Father God, let me die. I am weary of this life." Exhausted, he fell asleep and dreamed that an angel stood before him, saying, "Cut down the palm tree that grows near the spring and turn its fibers into a rope."

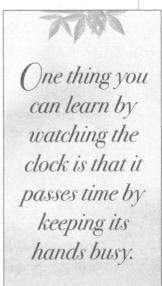

One thing you can learn by watching the clock is that it passes time by keeping its hands busy.

The hermit awoke and with great effort and many hours of toil, he felled the palm and made a coil of rope from its fibers. Again the angel appeared to him, saying, "I've seen you smiling every day as you worked. I can tell you are no longer weary of life. Go back into the world with your rope and find employment with it. Let it remind you toil is sweet."

Work not only benefits the mind and wallet, but the body, emotions, and soul. Work keeps all parts of the human machine in order. Just as machines rust out faster than they wear out, so, too, with people.

He also that is slothful in his work is brother to him that is a great waster.

Proverbs 18:9

Now there's even a "dial-a-prayer" for atheists. You call a number and nobody answers.

The story is told of a colony of mice who made their home at the bottom of a large upright piano. To them, music was frequent, even routine. It filled all the dark spaces with lovely melodies and harmonies.

At first the mice were impressed by the music. They drew comfort and wonder from the thought that Someone made the music—though invisible to them, yet close to them. They loved to tell stories about the Great Unseen Player whom they could not see.

Then one day an adventuresome mouse climbed up part of the way in the piano and returned with an elaborate explanation about how the music was made. Wires were the secret—tightly stretched wires of various lengths that vibrated and trembled from time to time. A second mouse ventured forth and came back telling of hammers—many hammers dancing and leaping on the wires. The mice decided they must revise their old opinions. The theory they developed was complicated, but complete with evidence. In the end, the mice concluded that they lived in a purely mechanical and mathematical world. The story of the Unseen Player was relegated to mere myth.

But the Unseen Player continued to play nonetheless.

*The fool hath said in his heart,
There is no God.*

PSALM 14:1

What must surely be one of the most frustrating conversations in history was reported in *Theatre Arts* magazine. A subscriber, desiring to report on a particular upcoming event in his community, dialed "Information" to get the magazine's telephone number.

The operator drawled, "Sorry, but there is nobody listed by the name of Theodore Arts."'

The subscriber insisted: "It's not a person; it's a publication. I want *Theatre Arts.*"

The operator responded, this time a little louder. "I told you, we have no listing for Theodore Arts in this city. Perhaps he lives in another city."

By now the subscriber was thoroughly peeved. "Confound it, the word is Theatre: T-H-E-A-T-R-E!"

He who thinks by the inch and talks by the yard deserves to be kicked by the foot.

The operator came back with certainty in her voice, "That—is not the way to spell Theodore."

Sometimes there's just no communicating with someone who refuses to hear you, who seems unwilling to understand your point of view, or who simply "doesn't get" what you are trying to say. Rather than give that person a real kick, however, better to hang up and try dialing someone who can hear you and does understand!

A fool's lips bring him strife,
and his mouth invites a beating.
PROVERBS 18:6 (NIV)

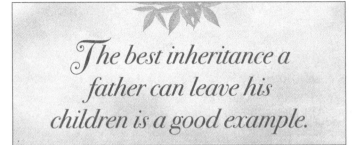

The best inheritance a father can leave his children is a good example.

A young woman relates that when she was a little girl, her father, an artist, would often be busy at his easel, mixing oils and painting on his big canvases while she sat nearby on the floor, working just as hard as he was with her own set of crayons and a coloring book.

Many a time, he would set his brushes aside, reach down, and lift her up onto his lap. Then he'd curl her little hand around one of his brushes, enfolding it with his own larger and stronger hand. And ever so gently, he would guide her hand and the brush, dipping it into the palette and mixing the burnt umbers and raw siennas, and then stroke the wet, shiny paint onto the canvas before them both.

The little girl watched in amazement as, together, they made something beautiful.

Little did this father know that he was giving his daughter skills that would bring great fulfillment to her life. Today, Joni Tada—a quadriplegic since a diving accident during her teen years—is still painting, but this time with a paintbrush in her mouth. Much of her earnings is channeled into ministry to help others. Her compassion, too, is a reflection of that shown by a loving, tender father.

As ye know how we exhorted and comforted and charged every one of you, as a father doth his children.

1 THESSALONIANS 2:11

Additional copies of this book and other
titles in the *God's Little Devotional Book* series
are available from your local bookstore.
Also look for our
Special Gift Editions in this series.

God's Little Devotional Book for Women
God's Little Devotional Book for Men
God's Little Devotional Book for Moms
God's Little Devotional Book for Dads
God's Little Devotional Book for Students
God's Little Devotional Book for Graduates
God's Little Devotional Book for Teachers
God's Little Devotional Book for Teens

If you have enjoyed this book,
or if it has impacted your life,
we would like to hear from you.
Please contact us at:

Honor Books
Department E
P.O. Box 55388
Tulsa, Oklahoma 74155

or by e-mail: info@honorbooks.com